D1412613

Writing Across the Curriculum

A Guide to Developing Programs

Susan H. McLeod
Margot Soven
editors

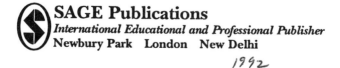

SAGE Publications
International Educational and Professional Publisher
Newbury Park   London   New Delhi

1992

For information address:

SAGE Publications, Inc.
2455 Teller Road
Newbury Park, California 91320

SAGE Publications Ltd.
6 Bonhill Street
London EC2A 4PU
United Kingdom

SAGE Publications India Pvt. Ltd.
M-32 Market
Greater Kailash I
New Delhi 110 048 India

Printed in the United States of America

Library of Congress Cataloging-in-Publication Data

Main entry under title:
Writing across the curriculum: a guide to developing programs/
(edited by) Susan H. McLeod, Margot Soven.
   p. cm.
  Includes bibliographical references.
  ISBN 0-8039-4599-X. — ISBN 0-8039-4600-7 (pbk.)
  1. English language—Rhetoric—Study and teaching.
2. Interdisciplinary approach in education. 3. Writing centers—
Administration. I. McLeod, Susan H. II. Soven, Margot.
PE1404.W6929 1992
808′ .042′ 071—dc20   92-28928

92 93 94 95 96 10 9 8 7 6 5 4 3 2 1

Sage Production Editor: Astrid Virding

Contents

Preface

The current collection of essays on writing across the curriculum (WAC) defines terms, presents helpful suggestions, even provides models for useful documents (everything from workshop evaluation forms to contracts for visiting consultants), and in short, makes everyone's work easier. As I read the manuscript, I found myself often agreeing, sometimes disagreeing, but always wishing that somehow this book had existed in 1974 when many of us were first embarking on the collegial enterprise now known as writing across the curriculum.

In the mid-seventies, a few colleges provided space and time for composition instructors to exchange ideas with colleagues in other disciplines. Often these conversations began as confrontations at meetings of curriculum committees, with instructors from "content" disciplines offering diatribes on the various failings of English 101. Carleton College (Northfield, Minnesota), under the academic leadership of Dean Harriet Sheridan, was the first institution that I know of to move the venue of these cross-curricular exchanges to the more civilized setting of a summer workshop. With modest funding from the Northwest Area Foundation, Carleton College instituted the first faculty writing workshops during the summers of 1974 and 1975. These workshops included undergraduates who were later designated "rhetoric fellows" and during the academic year were assigned to assist instructors of writing-intensive courses, performing the functions of what we today call writing fellows or writing associates. (In 1979, when Harriet

Sheridan became dean of the college at Brown University, she moved quickly to establish the well-known Brown Writing Fellows program, which she had already conceptualized and implemented at Carleton.)

In December of 1975, immediately after Mina Shaughnessy's stunning talk, "Diving In," at the meeting of the Modern Language Association (MLA) in San Francisco, I had the great good fortune to meet Harriet Sheridan on a cable car heading for Fisherman's Wharf. Before that cable car ride, I was one of many beleaguered and very junior composition instructors who had spent the previous autumn as flak catcher for the faculty's frustrations over student writing. After that cable car ride, I had in my possession something that could transform angst and indignation into productive collegial exchange. I had what we then called "The Carleton Plan." That plan had the seeds of all the basic principles of writing across the curriculum:

- Faculty writing workshops can create a nonhierarchical setting for real dialogue across disciplines.
- Curriculum change depends on intellectual exchange among faculty members.
- Faculty members must feel a sense of ownership in a WAC program.
- Collaboration is the key to success, among faculty members and among students.
- Undergraduates can be integrally involved in commenting on work-in-progress and can take a leadership role in a WAC program.
- Writing across the curriculum is built on a definition of writing as a complex process closely related to thinking.
- Writing across the curriculum helps students to learn subject matter as well as to improve fluency in writing.

In 1975, I was an assistant professor at a small, private, residential liberal arts college (Beaver). Today I am a dean at a large, urban commuter campus (Queens College/CUNY). As I approach the two-decade mark of thinking about writing across the curriculum in very different institutional settings, I conclude with some confidence that the movement has created momentum for real change in the academy. WAC is not merely a catch phrase to describe a fad of the seventies and eighties. The nineties are here, and writing across the curriculum is also here.

The current text will be enormously useful to readers who are now planning to initiate or expand writing across the curriculum on their own campuses. But let me take the privilege of the preface writer by adding a few suggestions on how best to use this book. I would strongly suggest listening to the cautionary words of several contributors who warn against the quick fix and urge careful study of individual institutional settings. Those who would change curriculum must become ethnographers of their home campuses. Advice in this book—or in this preface—must not become reified. The contributors to this volume are experienced enough to provide frequent road signs, warning against dogmatism and keeping readers focused on general principles that apply to a wide range of colleges and universities. When one author slips occasionally and says, "Never do such-and-such," several others will remind us never to say never. On the whole, this text provides a useful balance between individual perspectives and collective wisdom. We all have too much to do to waste our time reinventing wheels. But we cannot forget that all wheels—even those invented by others— must be carefully road tested on home terrain.

Although much has already been accomplished, much remains to be done. We still need a great deal more work on the place of the freshman English course in writing across the curriculum. Linda Peterson's excellent essay provides a starting point. But at far too many colleges and universities, a required first-year course often bears little connection to ambitious programs across the curriculum. Whether we like it or not, definitions of writing are communicated explicitly or implicitly in a required first-year course and those definitions become difficult to modify later. We ought to give more attention to freshman composition as a road map to understanding complex definitions of writing in college and beyond.

In 1981, in *Writing in the Arts and Sciences*, my co-authors and I presented a plan for freshman composition based on the concept of contextual variability. Our goal was to map a course that would prepare students to move gracefully and fluently from one setting to another, understanding differences, learning intellectual tact. Such tact, we thought, had the best chance of developing in students the confidence to question conventions and to challenge rules. Generic approaches to freshman composition depend on understanding this paradox: rebels are people who know the landscape and who can move easily through it. Those who would keep students ignorant of the academic landscape in the name of helping them to find their own rebellious voice do not understand much about guerrilla warfare.

Whether readers accept my way of connecting freshman composition with writing across the curriculum or Linda Peterson's approach or some other interesting mode of connection, we must develop institutional strategies to make this link. Yet, it is easier on most campuses to develop sophisticated approaches to writing almost anywhere except in the freshman composition program. On too many campuses we depend on underpaid, underprepared, and overworked adjuncts and graduate students to teach this definitive first-year course. We will have difficulty in making any productive intellectual connections until we address the larger issues of institutional priorities.

And, in fact, the most important theme in this collection is the connection between writing across the curriculum and reform in higher education. Changing institutional priorities so that freshman composition has resources and status depends on political and economic reforms. We have made very little progress in these areas. Yet, we are beginning to recognize that a coherent program of writing instruction is fundamental to reforming undergraduate education. As Shirley Strum Kenny, president of Queens College/CUNY, has remarked, "By any standards, in any institution where undergraduate education is important, writing across the curriculum is important." The implicit message in every essay in this collection is that writing across the curriculum is central to improving undergraduate education because WAC gets at fundamental principles of teaching and learning.

Learning occurs at the intersection of what students already know and what they are ready to learn. Writing to learn then becomes more than a way for students to learn new subject matter. Journals, letters, and other cognitive writing tasks also reveal to instructors and peers something of the writers' thought processes. Writing to learn becomes a way for instructors to learn about the individuals seated in that classroom. Who are they? What do they already know? What will connect them vitally to the abstractions in our lesson plans? Writing across the curriculum means involving students in their own learning, enabling students to establish dialogue with each other, with their textbooks, with documents of their culture, and with the world.

The years of faculty workshops, writing intensive courses, writing centers, and all the other projects described in this book have led us to understand that writing across the curriculum is about more than writing or reading or problem solving or critical thinking. Writing across the curriculum is a wedge into a reform pedagogy.

Farris and Smith in this volume talk of breaking into the safe pattern of lecture/test/lecture. Writing across the curriculum has broken through this pedagogic wall. Through responding to what students write in a variety of contexts, instructors can break through the undifferentiated mass of students in a lecture hall to connect with individuals in all their diversity.

Questions of text selection—the canon—often dominate our discussions of education for diversity. But the choice of assigned texts matters much less than our ability to connect those texts to the individual and differing minds, hearts, and life experiences arrayed before us in the classroom. Writing across the curriculum implies a set of powerful ways to make classrooms interactive. And an interactive classroom is one that is much more likely to respect difference.

Writing across the curriculum means incorporating student responses into teaching. When we take student responses into account, we give new meaning to teaching for diversity. A student born in Cambodia sits in a history classroom and writes a journal entry on U.S. immigration policy in the early twentieth century. An African-American born in Jamaica (Queens) writes a first draft of a critical analysis of *Huckleberry Finn*. An Italian-American born in Howard Beach works with the other two students in a peer group assigned to exchange individual approaches to solving calculus problems. The three students write acknowledgments for the interest and attention that the other students paid to their work-in-progress.

When classrooms in all disciplines focus on writing as a process of self-discovery and as a means for social interaction, we are really attending to the voices of diversity in our classes.

Yet, as we debate the expansion of the curriculum to encompass the globe, the most resilient enemy of WAC, fear over "coverage," gains strength. The first issue raised by wary faculty members had always involved the "C word." And the obsession with covering material is often more to bolster the professor's sense of self-esteem than it is to benefit students. Often we race through material, so that instructors who teach our students in later courses cannot accuse us of neglecting to mention something. If students don't remember what we said, well, that's their problem, but we can feel smug about covering the material. I'm still waiting for a T-shirt inscribed with the motto "I know that I taught it because I heard myself say it."

But in the nineties, as the academy plays a zero-sum game about what to cover, we need to work harder to communicate that WAC is a way of changing the rules of the game altogether. WAC provides practical means for reconceptualizing the goals of a course or of a curriculum plan. One of the most important outcomes of faculty writing workshops, as the essays in this volume confirm, is the reexamination of practices in light of redefined goals—goals that are realistically directed to student learning, not to abstract conceptions of what should be covered in a course. As I have said very often in writing workshops, the unexamined syllabus is not worth teaching; the unexamined curriculum is not worth implementing.

WAC is as timely in the nineties as it was in the seventies. But in addition to its resilience, WAC has also matured. We now have important works of scholarship to provide perspective for ongoing activities. One of the most significant scholarly works is *Writing in the Academic Disciplines, 1870-1990, A Curricular History* by David R. Russell. Russell demonstrates that attempts to incorporate writing instruction have always been linked with reform movements in higher education. The history of writing in the academic disciplines is a story of teachers committed to the principle that education must be respectful of students' abilities to be active participants in their own learning. More than a century of reform should encourage our efforts to make preface of what is past. *Writing Across the Curriculum: A Guide to Developing Programs,* to which this essay is preface, provides a road map for continuing reform.

ELAINE P. MAIMON
QUEENS COLLEGE/CUNY

ONE

Writing Across the Curriculum

An Introduction

SUSAN H. McLEOD

WAC IN THE NINETIES

It may seem strange, in the nineties, to publish a guide to developing writing across the curriculum (WAC) programs. After all, the WAC idea can be dated from the mid-seventies, when the first such programs were developed in the United States. The number of flourishing programs now seems legion; a 1985 survey by the Modern Language Association reported that 46% of all Ph.D.-granting institutions, 48% of all B.A./M.A.-granting institutions, and 28% of all two-year colleges had a WAC program of some sort (Kinneavy 362). More recently, a 1988 survey found that just under 50% of all postsecondary institutions in this country now have WAC programs (McLeod "Writing"). Writing across the curriculum has, in the space of a decade and a half, become a familiar part of the academic landscape.

Another way of looking at the national WAC picture, however, is that just over half of the colleges and universities in the United States do not yet have a WAC program, and the success of WAC elsewhere has made many of these institutions interested in developing such programs themselves. A 1991 videoconference titled "Issues and Conflicts in Writing Across the Curriculum," broadcast by the Public Broadcasting Service and produced by Robert Morris College, attracted the largest audience in the history of such videoconferences—401 downlink sites in 48 states and Mexico, with an estimated audience of 15,000.[1] This continuing interest in WAC is a testimonial to how successful the WAC movement has been.

But there are two significant differences in the way WAC programs are now being instituted, both of which have prompted the writing of this book. Ten years ago, it was common to get extramural funding and to bring in outside consultants to start a WAC effort. Today, except for a handful of programs funded by private agencies, most new programs must rely on internal funding. The fact that many institutions are now cutting rather than increasing their budgets means that outside consultants are sometimes out of the question. This volume, although it will not substitute for a visit from a WAC expert, will nevertheless answer some of the questions that would-be WAC directors might ask such a consultant.

The second difference in the way WAC programs are being started is clearly evident at the twice-a-year informational meetings held by the Board of Consultants of the National Network of WAC programs.[2] Ten years ago, the typical attendee at these meetings was a faculty member with a gleam in her eye who wanted advice about gaining administrative support for a WAC program; WAC was still very much a bottom-up phenomenon, led by a few dedicated faculty who had to contend with some administrative skepticism about the idea. Now, however, the situation seems almost reversed: Many attendees report that they have been sent by enthusiastic administrators who want to institute WAC, in spite of some faculty misgivings. (One rather desperate writing program administrator confided that her dean ordered her to "ram WAC down the faculty's throats, if necessary.") It is gratifying that the WAC idea now has wide administrative support, but as many contributors to this volume point out, faculty must own WAC programs in order for those programs to succeed. This book aims at giving interested administrators as well as faculty a guide to developing WAC programs that have both grass-roots and central administrative support.

The contributors to this volume are all involved in successful programs at a variety of institutions—large research institutions, small liberal arts colleges, comprehensive state universities, and community colleges. Most are long-time WAC directors; several have served as outside consultants to institutions starting WAC programs. Several serve on the Board of Consultants of the National Network of Writing across the Curriculum Programs. Some are or have been administrators, and some combine faculty and administrative duties. Because WAC programs are institution specific, readers are encouraged to skim all chapters and then focus on the sections discussing components that best fit with their own institutional structures and missions.

DEFINING WAC: WRITING TO LEARN AND LEARNING TO WRITE

In Chapter 2, Barbara Walvoord gives specific, practical advice about the first steps to take in starting a WAC program. Before taking any of those steps, however, would-be WAC directors need to define—for themselves as well as for their constituents—what the term means, because it often means different things to different people (see McLeod "Defining"). Recently, for example, I was accosted by an administrator from a small liberal arts institution who told me that the history of WAC programs needed to be rewritten, since his school had WAC before anyone else did: Faculty had been assigning term papers in every class for the last 25 years. Most WAC directors would argue with his notion of what defines a writing across the curriculum program. WAC does involve writing in all disciplines, but it certainly does not mean simply assigning a term paper in every class. Nor does it mean (as some faculty in the disciplines fear) teaching grammar across the curriculum. WAC programs are not additive, but transformative—they aim not at adding more papers and tests of writing ability, but at changing the way both teachers and students use writing in the curriculum.

To understand the changes WAC programs aim to make, it is useful to look at the theoretical bases for these programs. There are two approaches to WAC, approaches that are not mutually exclusive but complementary, as two of the main proponents of WAC have pointed out (Maimon, "Writing"; Fulwiler, "Friends"). We might think of them as being along a continuum in terms of the kinds of writing they advocate: in James Britton's terms, from *expressive* (to the self as audience) to *transactional* (to another audience, usually the teacher, for a grade). The first approach, sometimes referred to as *cognitive*, involves using writing to learn. This approach assumes that writing is not only a way of showing what one has learned but is itself a mode of learning—that writing can be used as a tool for, as well as a test of, learning. The work of James Britton and of Janet Emig undergird this approach, which is based on constructivist theories of education. Knowledge is not passively received, the theory goes, but is actively constructed by each individual learner; these constructions change as our knowledge changes and grows. One of the most powerful ways of helping students build and change their knowledge structures is to have them write for themselves as audience—to explain things to themselves before they have to explain them to someone else. In the curriculum, this approach advocates write-to-learn assignments such as journals and other ungraded writing assignments aimed at helping students think on paper (for examples of such assignments, see Fulwiler's *Journal Book*). The best-known program using this approach to WAC was developed by Toby Fulwiler at Michigan Technological University; it is described in Fulwiler and Young's book *Language Connections: Writing and Reading Across the Curriculum.*

It is important in discussing writing-to-learn assignments with faculty that we clarify what we mean by *learning*. One of the first questions a WAC director hears from colleagues is this: "What empirical evidence do you have that writing aids learning?" If one defines *learning* as simple recall of facts, the answer to that question is that we have little such evidence (Ackerman). In fact, if we are interested in having students only remember information, we would be better off instituting other kinds of assignments—memorization of mnemonic devices to aid recall, for example. But most of those involved in WAC efforts use the term *learning* as synonymous with *discovery*, as a way of objectifying thought, of helping separate the knower from the known; as a little girl once put it, "How can I know what I think until I see what I say?" (Wallas 106). We might think of writing to learn as a "knowledge-transforming" rather than a "knowledge-telling" task (see Bereiter and Scardemalia). For those interested in this question of how writing aids knowledge transformation, a recent article discusses how we might go about measuring such learning (Schumacher and Nash).

The second approach to WAC, sometimes termed *rhetorical*, involves learning to write in particular disciplines, or in what researchers have begun to think of as *discourse communities*. Although this approach does not exclude writing-to-learn assignments, it emphasizes more formal assignments, teaching writing as a form of social behavior in the academic community. The work of theorists on the social construction of knowledge, summarized by Kenneth Bruffee, underlies this approach. Knowledge in a discipline is seen not as discovered, but as agreed upon—as socially justified belief, created through the ongoing "conversation" (written as well as oral) of those in the field (see Maimon et al.). Our task in WAC programs is to help introduce students to the conventions of academic discourse in general and to the discourse conventions of particular disciplines—much as we would try to introduce newcomers into an ongoing conversation. (An example may clarify the notion of discourse communities. In writing about literature, we can use the present tense when quoting literary figures from the past—"Shakespeare says"—because for us the poet's words are not of an age but for all time. In writing about history, however, one uses the past tense: "Gibbon said." The words of those who write history are not taken by historians to be ageless, but must be considered in the context of the time in which they wrote.) Because this approach to WAC sees the discourse community as central to the process of writing as well as to the form of the finished product, it emphasizes collaborative learning and group work—attempting to model in the classroom the collaborative nature of the creation of knowledge. In the curriculum, this approach manifests itself in two ways: the freshman writing course that aims at introducing students to the general features of academic discourse and the writing-in-the-major (or writing-intensive) course that emphasizes the lines of reasoning and methods of proof for a particular discourse community. The best-known program taking this approach was established by Elaine Maimon at Beaver College, and is described in *Writing in the Arts and Sciences* and in "Talking to Strangers."

Writing across the curriculum may be defined, then, as a comprehensive program that transforms the curriculum, encouraging writing to learn and learning to write in all disciplines. Before discussing the possible components of such programs, it is worth reemphasizing the basic assumptions of WAC: that writing and thinking are closely allied, that learning to write well involves learning particular discourse conventions, and that, therefore, writing belongs in the entire curriculum, not just in a course offered by the English department. There is also an implicit assumption that WAC is a faculty-driven phenomenon, involving changes in teaching methods; WAC assumes that students learn better in an active rather than a passive (lecture) mode, that learning is not only solitary but also a collaborative social phenomenon, that writing improves when critiqued by peers and then rewritten. Faculty must see these as important and useful ways of teaching before they will institute them in their own classrooms; they will never be convinced by having WAC imposed on them— in fact, experience suggests that they will usually do their best to resist it. A WAC program needs strong administrative support, but it also has to be a bottom-up phenomenon, usually starting with a few committed faculty members and growing as others see how successful these faculty have been. Profound curricular and pedagogical change can come about as a result of a WAC program, but such change will not take place unless it comes from the faculty themselves. And change takes time. Successful WAC programs start slowly, phasing in various components over a period of years as a consensus develops that the program is useful (see McLeod *Strengthening*).

SETTING UP A PROGRAM: POSSIBLE COMPONENTS

Writing across the curriculum programs affect both faculty and students. The most successful programs are multifaceted, combining faculty development components with support systems and components that ensure curricular change. Which components are the best for your particular campus? The first step is to study your own institution, asking questions about the present administrative structure and budget (Which administrative office would support WAC on campus? What sort of budget is already in place for faculty development or curricular reform?), the curriculum (Where is writing already used in the disciplines? What kinds of writing courses exist inside and outside the English department?), any moves toward curricular reform (How could WAC figure into the reform of the general education curriculum? of restructuring a major, a department, a school?), and personnel (What faculty might be interested in a WAC program? Who is the best person to organize and spearhead the program?). After studying the institution and thinking about where a program could be built, housed, and funded, one should start talking to faculty. Barbara Walvoord, who has been advising faculty and administrators for nearly 20 years about starting WAC programs, deals with the issue of faculty dialogue in Chapter 2, "Getting Started." Whether *faculty* means the full professor at a liberal arts institution or a graduate teaching assistant at a research institution, those most involved in undergraduate instruction need to talk about how writing is taught and learned before instituting a program to improve that teaching and learning. Walvoord gives specific practical suggestions about how this dialogue can get started and how it can lead into productive program planning. She also gives advice to those who want to start a program after a hiatus.

The following chapters of the book deal with various components of WAC programs. It should be emphasized, however, that none of these components can exist entirely independently of the others. Successful WAC programs incorporate faculty and student support systems, curricular elements, and some administrative structure. Faculty development is an essential part of writing across the curriculum—almost all programs at one time or another hold workshops for faculty to discuss WAC concepts and to demonstrate techniques of assigning and evaluating student writing. In Chapter 3, Joyce Magnotto and Barbara Stout describe such workshops; discuss planning, funding, and evaluation; and offer advice about sustaining an ongoing series of workshops to engage faculty in productive discussion of writing and learning. As Magnotto and Stout point out, one of the most important things that a faculty workshop does is model WAC values for faculty by having them write themselves and share that writing with one another. The spirit of collegiality and sense of shared purpose that develop as a result of these workshops are important outcomes, especially at institutions where faculty morale needs a boost (see Weiss and Peich). In Chapter 4, Karen Wiley Sandler discusses WAC from an administrator's point of view. As a member of the French department at the University of Vermont she took part in Toby Fulwiler's WAC workshops; she has been an administrator at two other institutions, both of which had WAC programs. She discusses how administrators can support and nourish WAC efforts.

Once faculty are engaged in a WAC program, there are a number of possibilities—depending on the particular institution—for permanently integrating WAC into the curriculum, usually through some configuration of required courses. The curricular elements of WAC programs are various and institution specific, differing widely from campus to campus. The most obvious—and most neglected—course in WAC planning is freshman composition. Because WAC is thought of as existing apart from and outside of the English department, program planners often overlook one of the largest potential WAC populations. But this course is where our students get their first university-level writing instruction; it is only logical that any examination of possible WAC courses should begin at the beginning. Furthermore, any WAC program needs the support (or at least the benign neglect) of the English department to succeed. A lack of understanding of WAC principles in the department traditionally linked to writing instruction can eventually damage, perhaps even destroy, a WAC effort. In Chapter 5, Linda Peterson discusses a model that focuses on freshman composition as an introduction to academic writing, showing students how to analyze and then use the rhetorical conventions of various disciplines. In this model, the English department asks for help from other disciplines, help that those disciplines are usually very glad to give. Asking faculty for help in redesigning the introductory composition course can be the basis for subsequent WAC efforts.

Many WAC programs require students to take writing-designated courses outside the English department, either as part of general education requirements or as part of the students' major requirements. A common curricular element is the now-familiar writing-intensive (WI) course. Christine Farris and Raymond Smith (Chapter 6) define what *writing intensive* means and discuss models in which students are required to take a certain number of WI courses in their college careers, often in their major. They also suggest that a research component be connected to the consultation/follow-up model they propose for course design. The chapter by Christopher Thaiss (Chapter 7) defines the many purposes served by writing in general education courses and discusses ways to integrate writing into general education requirements across the disciplines. Because many schools are now in the process of revising their general education requirements, Thaiss describes a workshop model that lets WAC directors use the enthusiasm of curriculum planners to make writing an integral part of the new curriculum. Those who are thinking of starting a WAC program at large research institutions will find that there are models that work for their institutions as well; Joan Graham (Chapter 8) describes courses involving writing components (writing as an integrated part of a course), writing adjuncts (separate courses carrying less credit than the lecture to which it is attached), and writing links (autonomous courses attached to lectures and carrying equal weight). She also discusses the experiences of particular institutions with such models.

Once a WAC program is under way, support systems are needed to continue the program. In Chapter 9, Peshe Kuriloff describes one sort of model for faculty support in which the WAC director works closely with faculty in the disciplines on designing the course and assignments, consulting, collaborating, and sometimes even team-teaching the course. Faculty in the disciplines can be expected to assign and evaluate student writing, but unless their courses are very small, they cannot be expected to give the intensive one-on-one feedback to writers that well-trained tutors can give. In Chapter 10, Muriel Harris shows how a writing center is an essential support element for teachers and students alike. As Harris points out, a well-staffed writing center can be the hub of a WAC program. She also gives practical advice on how to set up and run a writing center, along with examples of such centers at a number of different institutions. A different model for support of faculty is discussed by Tori Haring-Smith (Chapter 11); the writing fellows programs she describes have been successful at Ivy League institutions, comprehensive state universities, and small liberal arts schools alike. In such programs, peer tutors do not work out of a writing center but are attached to particular courses. They respond to—but do not grade—drafts of student papers, giving students extensive feedback before the final version of the paper is due to the teacher. Finally, once program elements are in place WAC directors need to plan for the future. Margot Soven concludes with a chapter providing an overview of continuing WAC programs, discussing both the pleasures and the pitfalls of sustaining successful programs once they are launched.

A final word on starting WAC programs. As many of the contributors to this book would attest, being involved in WAC program development may have its frustrations, but it also has enormous rewards. As a WAC director, the best thing about WAC for me is what I have learned from my colleagues in other disciplines. It is all too easy for those of us in composition studies to subscribe to what Barbara Walvoord calls the *conversion model* of WAC—to think that we have The Word on words, and our task is to go forth to enlighten the heathen in other disciplines. Those who subscribe to this model will discover that they are the ones who become enlightened; when leading my first faculty workshops, I found that my idea of what constituted "good" writing was challenged and then expanded through lively discussion with chemists, political scientists, zoologists, historians, and engineers. WAC directors are—or must become—listeners as well as talkers, learners as well as facilitators of learning. Those who are starting WAC programs will find, I am sure, that what they learn from their colleagues in the disciplines about writing, learning, and teaching will be one of the most rewarding parts of their involvement in writing across the curriculum.

NOTES

1. For information on how to obtain a tape of this two-hour videoconference, contact William Sipple, Dean of Learning Resources, Robert Morris College, Narrows Run Road, Coraopolis, Pennsylvania 15108-1189. Dean Sipple's office also has a series of five half-hour faculty development resource tapes for use in workshops.

2. The network meetings are held at the National Council of Teachers of English Conference in November and the Conference on College Composition and Communication in March. For information about both these conferences, contact the National Council of Teachers of English, 1111 Kenyon Road, Urbana, Illinois 61801. The members of the Board of Consultants of the National Network of Writing Across the Curriculum Programs are Christopher Thaiss, coordinator, George Mason University; Toby Fulwiler, University of Vermont; Bernadette Mullholland Glaze, Fairfax County Public Schools (Virginia); Carin Hauser, Fairfax County Public Schools (Virginia); Joyce Magnotto, Prince George's Community College (Maryland); Susan McLeod, Washington State University; Lex Runciman, Oregon State University; Margot Soven, La Salle University; and Barbara Walvoord, University of Cincinnati. For further information about the network, contact Christopher Thaiss, Department of English, George Mason University, Fairfax, Virginia 22030.

WORKS CITED

Ackerman, John. "The Promise of Writing to Learn." Unpublished manuscript.

Bereiter, Carl, and Marlene Scardamalia. *The Psychology of Written Composition.* Hillsdale, NJ: Erlbaum, 1987.

Britton, James, et al. *The Development of Writing Abilities (11-18).* Urbana, IL: NCTE, 1975.

Bruffee, Kenneth A. "Collaborative Learning and the 'Conversation of Mankind.' " *College English* 46 (1984): 635-52.

Emig, Janet. "Writing as a Mode of Learning." *College Composition and Communication* 28 (1977): 122-28.

Fulwiler, Toby. "Friends and Enemies of Writing Across the Curriculum." Conference on College Composition and Communication. Chicago, 1990.

———. *The Journal Book.* Portsmouth, NH: Boynton, 1987.

Fulwiler, Toby, and Art Young, eds. *Language Connections: Writing and Reading Across the Curriculum.* Urbana, IL: NCTE, 1982.

Kinneavy, James. "Writing Across the Curriculum." *Teaching Composition: 12 Bibliographical Essays.* Ed. Gary Tate. Fort Worth: Texas Christian P, 1987. 353-77.

Maimon, Elaine. "Talking to Strangers." *College Composition and Communication* 30 (1979): 364-69.

———. "Writing Across the Curriculum: Reexamining False Dichotomies." Conference on College Composition and Communication. Chicago, 1990.

Maimon, Elaine, et al. *Writing in the Arts and Sciences.* Cambridge, MA: Winthrop, 1981.

McLeod, Susan. "Defining Writing Across the Curriculum." *WPA: Writing Program Administration* 11 (Fall 1987): 19-24.

———. "Writing Across the Curriculum: The Second Stage, and Beyond." *College Composition and Communication* 40 (1989): 337-43.

———, ed. *Strengthening Programs for Writing Across the Curriculum.* San Francisco: Jossey-Bass, 1988.

Schumacher, Gary M., and Jane Gradwohl Nash. "Conceptualizing and Measuring Knowledge Change Due to Writing." *Research in the Teaching of English* 25 (1991): 67-96.

Wallas, Graham. *The Art of Thought.* New York: Harcourt, 1926.

Weiss, Robert, and Michael Peich. "Faculty Attitude Change in a Cross-Disciplinary Writing Workshop." *College Composition and Communication* 31 (1980): 33-41.

TWO

Getting Started

BARBARA E. WALVOORD

So you want to start a writing across the curriculum program. You wonder

What are the first things to do?
What are possible models for shaping a program?
What sequence of activities should I and my colleagues plan?
Are there things we should *not* do? Pitfalls to avoid?
Where can we get resources?
What will the initial program cost?
How do we restart a WAC program after a hiatus?

This chapter addresses those questions.

FIRST: FACULTY DIALOGUE

WAC began, and still should begin, with faculty dialogue. Administrators and students should be included in certain parts of the dialogue. But the core of the enterprise is faculty dialogue.

Twenty-five years ago, one of the first WAC programs in the country began at Central College in Pella, Iowa. To occupy the void when my Chaucer seminar didn't "make," I circulated an invitation for any interested faculty from any discipline to meet every Tuesday afternoon of the semester from four to five p.m., in an empty seminar room, to talk about writing—how it was taught and learned on our campus and how we could improve both. There was a strong perceived need: from a faculty of 65, 14 volunteers from 8 disciplines showed up. We started, as many such groups still do, with a concern that our students could not write papers that met our expectations for thought, organization, or mechanics. We progressed, as most such groups do, to a wide-ranging exploration of language and learning in the classroom. During the semester, we read together from the available literature, discussed our concerns, examined samples of our own and our students' writing, and took turns buying the Oreos. The next year, other faculty who had heard of the meetings from their colleagues asked me to organize another one. After that, we thought we needed a longer workshop for still more faculty, so we explained to the dean what we thought we were doing, and he funded a summer workshop with a stipend of $75 per person for the week and all the Oreos we could eat. Eventually, we established an executive committee, politicked an assessment program through the faculty, wrote grants, got some released time for me as director, launched a writing center, and held regular seminars with bigger, grant-funded stipends and Dutch almond pastries. That WAC program, still going strong, has always had a basic foundation: faculty dialogue and faculty ownership.

When I interviewed in 1979 for a teaching position at Loyola College in Maryland, the administrators all knew what WAC was and that they wanted it, and they specifically asked me to begin a program. But I kept my mandate from the administration very quiet. Instead, I began by inviting faculty volunteers to gather each Tuesday afternoon between four and five p.m., to share Oreos and to discuss writing—how it was taught and learned on our campus and how we could improve both. Like the Central College program, Loyola's has been extraordinarily productive and long-lived, largely, I believe, because it began and continues as a faculty dialogue (Walvoord and Dowling).

One afternoon recently, a telephone caller introduced himself as the head of the English department at a school I won't name. "My dean says we have to start writing across the curriculum," he said in a puzzled tone. "Could you tell me what it is and how I should go about starting it?"

"Start," I told him, "with faculty dialogue." It can be done even if the initiator is an administrator and even at a large comprehensive or research university.

MODELS FOR WAC PROGRAMS

The Faculty Dialogue Model

The faculty dialogue model for starting a WAC program has these characteristics:

- Initiators move as quickly as possible to include, in a workshop setting that encourages dialogue, a range of faculty colleagues from various disciplines as well as teaching assistants, students, and others who will be affected. These people have a chance to shape and to own the program from the beginning. Initiators are careful to share power and ownership.
- The dialogue starts from needs and concerns that the faculty perceives and to which the faculty is willing to dedicate time and effort.
- Initiators, even if they have training in rhetoric or in English literature, do not view themselves as the only "experts" or as the teachers of the group but as colleagues in a mutual exchange, where everyone learns and everyone contributes.
- Changes in such areas as curriculum, schoolwide assessment, and writing centers arise from the dialogue. They usually happen after, and as a result of, the initial workshop(s).
- Administrators enter as participants in the dialogue, with their own kinds of insight. They also function as facilitators and as providers of resources for the program. They should not be seen as dictators who select WAC participants or decide the features of the program.

The goal of faculty dialogue is to explore language and learning on your campus. Faculty dialogue becomes the wellspring for changes in teaching and in other aspects such as curriculum and assessment.

Avoid the "Training Model,"
"Conversion Model," and
"Problem-Solution Model"

As you plan the initiation of your WAC program, you may unconsciously be working from models that will prove problematic. One mistake is to envision WAC as "training" for "untrained" faculty. The terms imply that there are certain skills or procedures that you will train faculty to implement, and then they will go out and do what they have been trained to do. Also problematic is the conversion model, which assumes that faculty in other disciplines are heathen who must be converted to the Right Way. Both these models lead to the faculty bashing that I find all too frequent among writing instructors in WAC programs—the assumption that faculty in other disciplines are all content with simply delivering boring lectures to their students, not asking them to write in meaningful ways, or not working with their writing and thinking processes. There may be some such faculty on your campus, but you're not likely to get them into your workshops anyway, and if you do, they're probably not going to change. The people who are going to accept your invitation for dialogue are the people who already have a concern about thinking and writing, who have been working hard at the task of teaching, and who have much to offer as well as much to learn from others. What they need is time to think about writing and learning; resources that will help them think productively; and0 a supportive community to help them think, plan, and change. That's what writing instructors also need. If you are a writing instructor, be ready to listen and learn from your colleagues in other disciplines as well as to share with them what you know about writing and learning.

Another reason the training or conversion models won't work is that teaching methods suggested in WAC seminars may work very differently for different teachers, as has been demonstrated by studies of teachers in various disciplines who were using methods suggested to them through WAC seminars (Langer and Applebee; Marshall; Walvoord and McCarthy). The classroom teachers themselves are going to have to observe their own students and adapt what they learn in the WAC workshops to their own situations.

The problem-solution model is also dangerous. There may be problems on your campus that the WAC group will define and try to address, but if WAC is seen only as a solution to a particular problem, then everyone expects that, if WAC is successful, the problem will be solved and WAC can end. On the contrary, WAC helps people grow. We could have WAC workshops for faculty on every campus every year until the end of the world, because teachers always can be helped by dialogue with colleagues; always need to keep up with new research and theory about writing, thinking, and learning; and always need help in observing and learning what methods will work best in their own classrooms.

SEQUENCE OF ACTIVITIES FOR BEGINNING A WAC PROGRAM

Figure 2.1 proposes a sequence of activities for initiating WAC.

The Initiator

The initiator may directly plan the first workshop, especially if he or she is a veteran faculty member with good connections on campus, if other faculty trust the initiator's planning, and if the initiator, alone, can effectively recruit faculty into the first workshop. The initiator should consult widely, be careful not to push a rigid, preconceived outcome or agenda for the workshop, and avoid the trainer or "missionary" stance. The advantages are that an initiator can often move quickly and efficiently to get the first workshop off the ground. The disadvantage is that potential allies and participants might be more committed if they had been part of the original planning.

The Initial Planning Committee

Alternately, the initiator may choose not to plan immediately the first workshop but instead to invite a temporary planning committee to launch the WAC program. The committee, then, is where dialogue begins. The initial planning committee should include faculty from various disciplines, as well as others who are affected and who can make a contribution—administrators, staff,

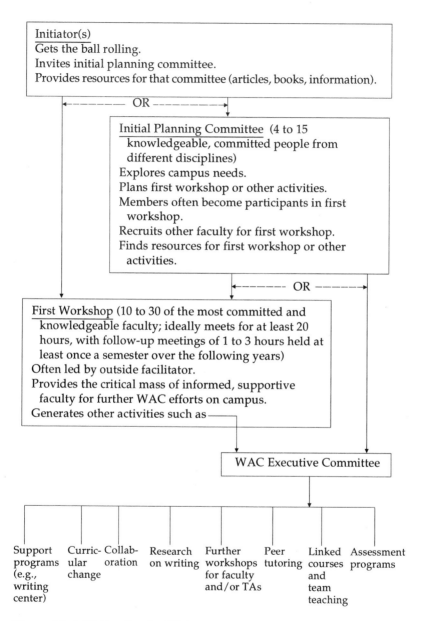

Figure 2.1. Initiating Faculty Dialogue

students, and teaching assistants (TAs). Its members should be the most knowledgeable and committed people on campus; do not use the committee appointment to try to make an ally out of a hostile or disinterested colleague. The committee may eventually evolve into a permanent executive committee, but it can begin as a temporary body, invited informally by the initiator. This committee model may be slower and more cumbersome than direct action by the initiator but has the advantage of enhancing faculty ownership and investment in the program. It's a very good option if the initial impetus for WAC comes from a person who is new to the faculty, who holds a staff or administrative position, or who might be seen by colleagues as an empire builder who needs some checks and balances.

Recruit people *in person* for the initial planning committee. Your invitation can focus on whatever issues or concerns you think are most compelling to your colleagues. You may not even mention the term *WAC* at this point, if you think it would be misleading or unfamiliar. You might invite people to a meeting to consider "students' writing and thinking" or "critical thinking" or "the place of writing in the upcoming core curriculum revision" or "problems with the freshman writing assessment program" or whatever else has been or might be the impetus for people to start reexamining writing and learning on your campus. It's fine to begin with what the campus perceives as a problem, provided the discussion broadens to the nature of language and learning, with the WAC literature as one resource among others.

You may find it more politic to work through an existing body to form the committee. I've known initial planning committees that were spawned by the faculty senate or by committees on core programs or on the freshman experience.

If you are the person who calls the initial planning meeting, you may act as facilitator and resource person, but you should be careful not to dominate. Your stance should be that anyone present at the meeting has worthwhile ideas to contribute, not that these are learners and you are the teacher.

The nature of the committee depends on the situation. I've seen initial planning committees the members of which are already quite knowledgeable about WAC and who, within a month or two, generate a plan and begin implementation. On the other hand, I've seen initial planning committees that spend several months or a year in dialogue among themselves, reading and discussing WAC literature, attending conferences, visiting other schools, and sharing their own and their students' writing, and finally emerging with a plan for further workshops or other curricular and programmatic activities. In this case, the committee takes on aspects of a first workshop. For example, I visited a campus where the planning committee was composed of 16 faculty from a variety of disciplines as well as an assistant to the academic vice president. The committee had been called together by two faculty members in disciplines outside English, with the blessing of the academic vice president. The group had been meeting, reading, discussing, and planning for a year. At their invitation, I led a two-day workshop just for members of the committee, helping them build on what they'd already learned. We focused both on their own teaching and also on long-range plans for the WAC program. The next year, I went back to lead a three-day workshop, which the committee had planned for an wider and different group of faculty, this time focusing only on teaching, not on program planning. After this workshop, the original planning committee decided to restructure as an elected standing committee, smaller in size, with regular rotation. Some new graduates of the first workshop were elected, so the committee got a new shot of energy. They drew up a five-year plan, including further faculty workshops, a writing center, liaison with local kindergarten to 12th-grade (K-12) schools, and a WAC director with released time.

Activities and pace of the initial planning committee, therefore, may differ according to the nature of the committee. At the early planning meetings, the initial planning committee might do any of these things:

1. Elect a chair who will convene and chair future meetings.
2. Discuss whether the committee has the members and the representation it needs. Would you like to add students? TAs? administrators? Writing center director? Other faculty?
3. Define key terms, such as *WAC, critical thinking, writing,* and *assessment.*
4. Distribute resources for reading and later discussion.
5. Plan trips for committee members to other campuses and to conferences to discover more about WAC and about what other schools are doing.

6. Identify key concerns about learning, teaching, and writing, both in your classrooms and on the campus at large.
7. Plan for each committee member to bring an assignment he or she has used, together with two student papers written in response to the assignment. Each person explains the goals of the assignment, the strengths and weaknesses of the students' writing, and how she or he might do this assignment next time. This exercise helps committee members get a sense of others' goals and teaching methods, leads to dialogue about teaching and learning, and helps pinpoint issues.
8. Plan the first workshop.
9. Identify specific faculty who might be interested in the first workshop and plan how to recruit them.

If you are the initiator who convened the committee, it may work perfectly well simply to assume that you will chair the initial planning committee. However, you may ask the committee to elect a chair, particularly in certain circumstances—if, for example, you are in the English department and you wish to communicate that WAC is not solely an English department program; you are an administrator and wish to encourage faculty ownership of the program; you are a new faculty member, an adjunct, or a staff member, and you believe the committee needs the clout it can achieve if chaired by a veteran faculty member; or if you are afraid you may be seen as an empire builder and wish to demonstrate your democratic motives. I have worked on several WAC committees at different schools where someone else was the chair. I served as a source of information and resources because I had read widely in WAC literature and because I directed a grant or administered a program that had resources. You don't need to be the official chair to play these other important roles.

The initial planning committee can be a short-lived, temporary group that launches the program. Some of its members may eventually be members of the long-term WAC executive committee, but you may want to hold the first workshop before you set the governance of WAC too firmly, because often your best people emerge from the first workshop, sometimes in ways that surprise you. Also, committee membership is one good way to begin to give the graduates of the first workshop a chance to become owners and spokespeople for the WAC program.

The First Workshop

On many campuses, the first thing the initiator or the initial planning committee plans is a workshop for 10 to 30 faculty volunteers from various disciplines. Only with caution and after considerable thought should the committee move directly to instigate programmatic or curricular changes without introductory faculty workshops. Throughout the history of the WAC movement, the interdisciplinary faculty workshop has been the basis of the WAC movement, providing the yeast of understanding and commitment that leavens the curricular and programmatic elements of the WAC program.

As with the initial planning committee, do not invite into the first workshop your most intransigent colleagues in an attempt to win them over. On every campus there are three types of faculty: some who are already sympathetic or involved, a large middle group who potentially can be enlisted, and a group who are opposed or indifferent and who probably will never change. Begin by organizing and informing the most interested group so they become articulate and knowledgeable implementers and spokespeople. Then recruit the middle group. Leave the intransigents alone and try not to get them into workshops. Otherwise, their objections, voiced in the group, will co-opt the group's time and attention, preventing the group from getting on with the business that most people present are ready for. This means, in effect, never have a workshop that faculty are *required* to attend. You can use a required faculty meeting for a 10-minute announcement or an hour-long preview of the WAC workshops, but no more.

A typical phone call I received recently illustrates one ill-advised way to plan the first workshop. "We're starting a WAC program," the faculty member said, "and the academic vice president says we can have most of the day of faculty orientation in the fall. Could you come and do a workshop from 10 a.m. to 3 p.m. for our entire faculty?" This proposal is studded with problems. First, faculty are, if not required, at least strongly expected to attend, so there's a captive audience. What's likely to happen is that a few faculty will be hostile, and their objections will take up the attention of the group. Second, the length of this workshop is awkward. It's too short for getting past initial misconceptions and exploring language and learning in any depth. Thus you are not likely to see lasting classroom changes in teachers as a result of this sort of workshop. Yet you've spent a considerable sum bringing in an outside consultant. The academic vice president is likely next year to say, "We did WAC last year; now we need something else." So that's the end of the resources for WAC, and you haven't gotten any bang for your buck. It would be far better to use 5 or 10 minutes of the general faculty orientation meeting for advertising, or an hour for previewing a later workshop that would enroll 10 to 30 volunteers and that would last at least two days (three days or more would be even better). That workshop could start with the concerns of faculty who were ready to move forward; it could help those faculty make lasting classroom changes; and it could create a knowledgeable and committed group who would then yield members for an executive committee, presenters for further workshops, and supporters for other changes on campus.

PITFALLS TO AVOID

In addition to the dangerous workshop scenario I've just outlined, the following activities, if launched before or just after the first workshop, may be problematic (they may, however, be appropriate later on as the program matures):

1. Administering a facultywide questionnaire or survey about current attitudes or teaching practices.
2. Writing or adopting a booklet for your campus that sets standards for mechanics in student papers or that offers advice for grading and writing comments on student papers in various disciplines.
3. Instituting a writing test for students that will be required for graduation.

The questionnaire that asks faculty about their current practices can be very threatening to faculty, intimating that the WAC program is going to nail them as shirkers and/or ask them to do more work. Faculty tend to fear that such a survey, despite your assurances of anonymity, may affect their standing with administrators; their reputation among other faculty; or even their tenure, promotions, and salary. Furthermore, the survey implies a problem-solution model of WAC. The intimation is that if the survey results show the faculty to be incompetent, workshops will be instituted to change them. The success of the workshop will be judged by its ability to effect change in the survey results, and thus "fix" the problem.

Hanging the success of the WAC program on its ability to change results of a facultywide survey is dangerous for two reasons: first, though you certainly can get quantitative measures of the significant changes that faculty in the workshop institute as a result of the workshop, the survey cannot capture all, or even the most important, changes that take place—for example, changes in faculty attitudes toward students, changes in the tone and content of what they say to students about writing, and their renewed interest in teaching. Second, it's hard to get survey results that reflect significant changes in a faculty as a whole as a result of workshops, because the most intransigent 20% of faculty does not even enroll for a workshop. A far better way of measuring changes wrought by the workshop is to ask faculty enrolled in the workshops, on day one, to complete a questionnaire or to describe their current teaching practices. At the end of the workshop, have them complete the questionnaire again, but also have them write about how they've changed, perhaps using the early questionnaire as a reference to remind them of where they were. You are likely, then, to get specific information about significant changes that a questionnaire would have difficulty in capturing.

I would also advise against starting a WAC program by creating a booklet for the entire faculty that lays out campuswide standards or methods for grading student papers. Nor is it wise to begin by choosing a commercially published handbook that everyone will use and refer to. These initiatives are likely to give faculty and students the inaccurate impression that WAC is only a matter of grammar and punctuation, and/or that WAC asks faculty to write more comments on student papers, and/or that the chief focus of WAC is grading finished written products. Those are some major misconceptions you'll have to fight anyway, all through the WAC program; there's no sense making your job harder by starting on that tack. You may eventually decide to publish or adopt such a book, but it should be done only within the context of other activities and only by a knowledgeable, well-workshopped group of faculty that recognizes, and can communicate to other faculty, that grammar and punctuation are only part of the broader concerns of writing and learning.

A good early project, however, might be a booklet of writings by faculty who have taken the first workshop. In the booklet, those faculty report what they learned and how they now teach, as a result of the WAC program. Successful booklets of that nature are Gestwicki, Griffin, Smith and Watson, Thaiss, and *Undercurrents*. Such reports of the workshop can also be disseminated through a newsletter to faculty. One of the most long-lived and useful newsletters distributed to a number of schools is *Crosscut*. Anyone interested in starting one could write to other schools for samples; the membership list of the National Network of Writing Across the Curriculum Programs identifies schools that publish WAC newsletters.[1] Another useful booklet project that might result after one or more workshops is a booklet for students, in which the faculty of each department write to students about the importance of writing in that discipline and about how teachers in that discipline work with writing. Both Central College and Loyola College have such booklets. At Loyola, all students buy it as a text in their required freshman composition course (Bredihan and Mallonee).

The third way not to begin a WAC program is by instituting a test to make sure that no incompetent writers graduate from your school or become juniors. This test is likely to concentrate, or be perceived among faculty to concentrate, on grammar and punctuation, again giving a wrong impression of WAC. If the test does not concentrate on grammar and punctuation, some faculty may want it to. Moreover, collegewide testing of writing reinforces the notion that writing is context free and can be fairly tested by gathering students in a gym some Saturday morning and asking them to write on a topic of supposedly general knowledge for an unseen audience of teachers who gather on the following Saturday morning to decide who passed and who failed. Recent research and theory in writing has seriously questioned all these premises. For example, Frank Sullivan has investigated the complexity of raters' judgments of writers in these situations. Issues of whether the test is fair to various races, socioeconomic classes, and ethnic groups are extremely problematic. Testing all students to make sure they are competent writers before graduation may sound straightforward, but it is highly complex, questionable in many aspects, legally dangerous unless you have a well-validated test, and it consumes many resources that might, instead, be used directly to help faculty improve classroom teaching so that every student could benefit.[2]

FINDING RESOURCES

Grants

It's a mistake to think that you can't have an effective WAC program unless you get a grant, but on the other hand, you should not overlook grant possibilities. Grants for traditional WAC programs are no longer available from national foundations that funded them in the past—foundations such as the National Endowment for the Humanities or the Fund for the Improvement of Postsecondary Education. Some smaller, specialized, or local foundations, however, may still be possibilities; your school's grants officer can help you. Local donors are also possible; most schools won't let you approach them on your own—you should work through your development office. What happens, in my experience, is that the development office decides (or not) to give you a donor they know can be tapped. They may not give you that donor if their higher priority is to tap that donor for the current capital campaign. Thus sometimes you need the provost or president to help you persuade the development office that the WAC program should be assigned a donor. Also, help them think of donors who might not give to the capital campaign but who would give to WAC—for example, the local newspaper, publisher, or bookstore.

Another option is to shape your basic enterprise—helping teachers with language, teaching, and learning—into a grant proposal that someone will fund. Programs that address critical thinking, cultural literacy, or whatever the current buzzword comes to be, can be shaped to deal usefully with writing as part of their concern for language, teaching, and learning.

Collaboration With Other Schools

A common mistake is to think that if you can't get a grant you have to go it alone. Collaboration with other schools and organizations can provide important resources.

Piggybacking on someone else's conference is one route. A common way of initiating WAC is to send one or two faculty members to a conference. Popular conferences have been the Conference on College Composition and Communication (the key conference for college writing teachers) and the conference of the National Council of Teachers of English (which draws a more varied crowd that consists largely of K-12 teachers with some community college and college teachers). If you attend either of these two conferences, be sure to go to the session of the National Network of Writing Across the Curriculum Programs mentioned earlier. There, you will have a chance to see some national WAC leaders who might be potential workshop leaders, a chance to discuss your own situation in small groups that these leaders facilitate, and a chance to join the National Network and receive its directory. The chief advantage of the conferences is the chance to see a variety of speakers. The disadvantage is that most presentations are pitched at professionals in writing. Faculty from other disciplines may find some presentations full of theory and jargon that doesn't mean much and may feel like ducks on a chicken farm.

The special-topic conference is another option. For three or four days, participants gather to hear speakers and to engage in workshop sessions on issues related to a particular topic. It is important to find out whether the conference is pitched at researchers and theorists or at practitioners. An example is the annual National Institute on Issues in Teaching and Learning at the University of Chicago. Find others advertised in current issues of *College Composition and Communication*.[3]

The most directly practical conference is the one that specifically addresses WAC. The longest-lived such conference that I know of is "Wild Acres," which has been organized by Sam Watson at the University of North Carolina at Charlotte.[4] Here, faculty from UNCC and a variety of other schools attend a four-day WAC workshop at a lovely Carolina mountain retreat. Interchange among participants is much easier than at the typical Hyatt Regency where the annual professional meetings are held. It's a more interactive and focused look at WAC than you would find at a typical professional conference. The workshop is led by nationally known WAC leaders. A workshop such as this is the best introductory experience I know of for faculty members from all disciplines who are considering a WAC program.

A third option is to send one or more of your school's faculty to a workshop that some other school is giving for its own faculty. I've led a number of workshops at schools where one or two faculty from neighboring schools will have heard about the workshop through the grapevine and asked if they could attend. It helps them see what a WAC workshop looks like, it gives them a chance to see the workshop leader in action and decide if they might want to get that person for their own workshop, and it may be a prelude to useful collaboration between the WAC programs at the two schools. Call your neighbors and ask if any of them is doing a WAC workshop. Or contact schools that are listed in the directory of the National Network of Writing Across the Curriculum Programs already mentioned or listed in the back of McLeod's *Strengthening Programs for Writing Across the Curriculum*.

Another option is to combine resources with nearby schools. A good example is the Baltimore Area Consortium for Writing Across the Curriculum (BACWAC). In its first few years, the consortium ran intensive workshops that enrolled faculty from a variety of local colleges, community colleges, and high schools. Each school paid $200 per participant for a 30-hour workshop. Then, using the annual $75 membership fees that each school paid, we established a structure through which member schools could hire the best of those workshop graduates as presenters for workshops on their own campuses, again at minimal cost (Walvoord and Dowling).

WHAT WILL A WAC PROGRAM COST?

The three largest expenses that a WAC program is likely to encounter are (1) released time for the director, (2) the cost of outside speakers and workshop leaders, and (3) possible stipends for workshop participants. The last two are discussed in the next chapter, on faculty workshops. The issue of released time for the WAC director deserves a further word here.

Initiators of WAC programs often work without remuneration as a service to the institution. They need to get *credit* for their effort within the university's reward system. They should, from the outset, keep accurate records of the time they spend on WAC, both for their own benefit and as a basis for the committee's later planning about how much released time will be required.

After the initial year, the ongoing executive committee probably will need to help the director get released time. Often the best way is for the committee to draw up a two-, three-, or five-year plan for WAC, detailing the resources that will be needed, including released time for the director. A good example is the five-year plan of Chesapeake College.[5] In estimating released time, early records about time spent organizing initial workshops or other activities will be valuable. If you need some idea of what schools of your type are providing in released time, contact schools like yours listed in the National Network of WAC Programs directory or in McLeod, mentioned earlier.

If, despite your best efforts, no released time is forthcoming, the program will proceed more slowly and in a more limited way. Probably the best arrangement is a large executive committee, the members of which can share the workload. It helps if the committee can be assigned a student helper, secretary, or administrative assistant who can do at least some of the work of organizing workshops, keeping records, handling correspondence, advertising WAC activities, and so on. Keep careful records of how much time committee members and assistants spend, and of initiatives that the committee would like to undertake but that would require a director with released time. Armed with these records, periodically repeat your requests for a director with released time.

RESTARTING A WAC PROGRAM
AFTER A HIATUS

Increasingly, I am getting calls from people who are restarting a WAC program after what they, at least, view as a hiatus. Typically, the caller will say, "We had some workshops here about seven or eight years ago, but nothing much has been done in the last few years, and we want to get started again."

The advice about starting with faculty dialogue as well as the models discussed in this chapter all apply, but there's the additional consideration of how to integrate the earlier start into the new start. The most obvious dangers are that you will ignore people from the earlier round who could help you or that you will unintentionally offend them and/or their friends. The problem of ignoring competent former participants in workshops can be remedied by making sure you inquire and publicize widely, so that you can identify all these veterans. Look for records and talk to a variety of people, so you are familiar with past history. A newly hired writing center director at one school recently called to find out whether I would meet with him to help plan a WAC effort on his campus. "Oh," I said, "I did a WAC workshop at your college about seven years ago." He was astonished—"You did?" He was not aware of the earlier effort or of the roles of its leaders, most of whom were still on campus. He needed to do some talking to people on his own campus before he came to me.

Once you have found out about earlier efforts, you must think carefully about how to manage the situation, especially if you are new. I saw this situation recently: A WAC workshop led by an outside leader had been organized about six years before, by a faculty member still on campus. This faculty member was respected for her accomplishments and intelligence but widely viewed as a difficult person to work with. There had been no effective follow-up to the initial workshop, and the program had lapsed. Now a new English department faculty member had been expressly charged at his hiring to restart WAC. He began wisely, as a new faculty member, by talking and listening. He countered his own status as new kid on the block by quickly appointing an initial planning committee. He decided not to invite the former organizer to serve on the initial planning committee, but he did invite a veteran of the earlier workshop who was well regarded on campus. Advertising for the workshop, he took care to separate this new effort from the old but also to acknowledge the contribution of the former workshop, but without naming names. The advertisement noted that the earlier workshop had laid a theoretical grounding, but the forthcoming workshop would focus on practical applications and was open to those who had or had not attended the earlier workshop. So far, so good. My mistake as the invited workshop leader was that, though I saw that phrasing in the advertisement, I did not ask who the earlier organizer had been and whether that person was still on campus. She showed up in the first workshop session, but at first I had no idea who she was. At the first opportunity, she sharply attacked my approach, making sure to work in the fact that she had initiated WAC years ago on campus. Fortunately, we were able quickly to turn the discussion into positive channels and she was able to contribute positively to the rest of the workshop without dominating or disrupting it. Still, there were some tense moments not only for me but, to judge by the "here-we-go-again" looks on the faces of the other faculty, for them as well. Ideally, I think, it would have been good if the WAC director had alerted me to the possible presence of this former organizer, so that I could have immediately acknowledged her presence, her role in initiating WAC on that campus, and her value as a resource to the group. Then she would not have had to launch an attack to get her special status as an "expert" acknowledged. Perhaps even better, if there had been time, I might have had breakfast that morning with all the veterans of the earlier workshop to hear from them what had been done there. That would have recognized their experience and their special role, offered the former leader a chance to validate her approach, and established some trust between us. We needed, in other words, a little faculty dialogue.

So then, in summary, whether starting or restarting, whether on a large campus or a small one, with a grant or without, in the seventies or the nineties, WAC begins with faculty dialogue—a dialogue about language use in the classroom; a dialogue about thinking, reading, discussing, writing, teaching, and learning; a dialogue that we hope will continue, perhaps in different shapes and under different banners, on all of our campuses as long as there are learners in our classrooms.

NOTES

1. To obtain the membership list, send $5 to Chris Thaiss, Department of English, George Mason University, Fairfax, Virginia 22030.

2. For help and information about assessment of students, contact the National Testing Network, City University of New York, 535 East 80th Street, New York, New York 10021; phone: 212-772-5175.

3. For the National Institute on Issues in Teaching and Learning at the University of Chicago, write to the Office of Continuing Education, 5835 South Kimbark, Judd 207, Chicago, Illinois 60637. If your library does not carry *College Composition and Communication*, write to the National Council of Teachers of English, 1111 Kenyon Road, Urbana, Illinois 61801.

4. For further information, write Department of Religious Studies, UNCC, Charlotte, North Carolina 28223.

5. For further information, write to Gail Bounds at Chesapeake College, Wye Mills, Maryland 21679.

WORKS CITED

Breihan, John, and Barbara Mallonee, eds. *Loyola College Writing Handbook: A Guide to Writing in All the Disciplines.* Baltimore: Loyola College. Phone 410-323-1010; or write Breihan or Mallonee at Loyola College, Baltimore, MD 21210.

Central College. Annual catalog. Dept. of Admissions, Pella, IA 50219. Phone 515-628-5286; speak to Ellen Heiting.

Crosscut. English dept., California State University, 5500 University Parkway, San Bernardino, CA 92407.

Gestwicki, Ron, ed. *The Writing/Learning Process: Getting Started.* University of North Carolina at Charlotte, 1984. Phone 704-597-4598; cost $5.

Griffin, C. Williams. *Final Report to the National Endowment of the Humanities, Grant ED 20127-83.* Virginia Commonwealth University, Richmond, VA, 1985. Write C. Williams Griffin at VCU, Dept. of English.

Langer, Judith A., and Arthur N. Applebee. *How Writing Shapes Thinking: A Study of Teaching and Learning.* NCTE Research Report #22. Urbana, IL: National Council of Teachers of English, 1987.

Marshall, James D. "Process and Product: Case Studies of Writing in Two Content Areas." *Contexts for Learning to Write: Studies of Secondary School Instruction.* Ed. Arthur N. Applebee. Norwood, NJ: Ablex, 1984. 149-68.

McLeod, Susan, ed. *Strengthening Programs for Writing Across the Curriculum.* San Francisco: Jossey-Bass, 1988.

Smith, Janet, and Sam Watson, eds. *What's Happening With Writing at UNC Charlotte: Writing Intensive Developments in Context.* Charlotte: University of North Carolina at Charlotte, 1990. Write Stan Patton, UNC Charlotte, Dept. of English, Charlotte, NC 28223; $5 to $7.

Sullivan, Francis J. "Placing Texts, Placing Writers: Sources of Readers' Judgments in University Placement-Testing." NCTE Promising Researcher Report. Unpublished manuscript. Philadelphia: Temple U, 1987.

Thaiss, Christopher, ed. *Writing to Learn: Essays and Reflections on Writing Across the Curriculum.* Dubuque, IA: Kendall/Hunt, 1983.

Undercurrents: Conversations About Writing by Teachers at All Levels. Write editor Steve Fishman, Department of Philosophy, University of North Carolina at Charlotte, Charlotte, NC 28223.

Walvoord, Barbara E., and H. Fil Dowling, Jr., with John R. Breihan, Virginia Johnson Gazzam, Carl E. Henderson, Gertrude B. Hopkins, Barbara Mallonee, and Sally McNelis. "The Baltimore Area Consortium." *Programs That Work: Models and Methods for Writing Across the Curriculum.* Ed. Toby Fulwiler and Art Young. Portsmouth, NH: Boynton, 1990. 273-86.

Walvoord, Barbara E., and Lucille P. McCarthy, with contributions by Virginia Johnson Anderson, John R. Breihan, Susan Miller Robison, and A. Kimbrough Sherman. *Thinking and Writing in College.* Urbana, IL: National Council of Teachers of English, 1991.

THREE

Faculty Workshops

JOYCE NEFF MAGNOTTO
BARBARA R. STOUT

Writing across the curriculum is realized through changes in faculty and student assumptions about writing. Faculty workshops are an excellent medium for such changes because they integrate theory and practice in an experiential environment. In WAC workshops participants learn to use multiple drafts, to share their writing, and to respond to each other's writing. They discover that the WAC movement is grounded in scholarship and research. They reexamine pedagogies in light of WAC values: writing as a means of learning; the interdependence of composing processes and written products; the merits of different kinds of writing; respect for the ideas of every writer; and an appreciation of writing as socially, cognitively, and rhetorically complex.

Many faculty come to WAC workshops thinking of school writing as primarily research papers, essay exams, and laboratory reports because these were the assignments they wrote as students. Some faculty are not sensitive to the convolutions of people's writing processes and the courage it takes to share a piece of writing. In a workshop setting, faculty try different kinds of writing and read one another's efforts, learning firsthand that assignments must be carefully designed with purposes clear to both faculty and students. They are reminded that sharing writing can be threatening even with supportive readers. They learn methods that make the task of responding to writing less difficult. Those who participate in WAC workshops return to the classroom with a fuller sense of the multiple roles that writing plays in teaching and learning. Furthermore, in a workshop context, a spirit of collegiality develops into a powerful force for sustaining WAC. Faculty talk about the discourses of different disciplines with colleagues outside their department, with colleagues whose offices are across campus, and with colleagues who also struggle with writing assignments. As Barbara Walvoord makes clear in Chapter 2, such collegial dialogue is a cornerstone of strong WAC programs.

Because the workshop dynamic models WAC values, encourages reflexive pedagogy, and fosters faculty dialogue, we believe it is a powerful stimulus for changing faculty assumptions about writing. And while we know that not all WAC programs call for faculty workshops, we contend that some form of faculty development (whether for tenured professors or teaching assistants, whether through workshops, speakers, symposia, or conferences) is a critical ingredient in WAC programs. For those of you who are working on faculty development, we hope this chapter will help you with workshop planning, funding, and evaluation, and with making workshops an integral part of your WAC program.

PLANNING WAC WORKSHOPS

Before you and your fellow WAC advocates plan even a first workshop for your faculty, we suggest sketching out a preliminary design for the WAC program as a whole (see Figure 2.1). That means considering questions such as the following: What do you want WAC to achieve at your institution during the next three years? the next five years? Are you aiming for changes in individual classrooms? curricular change? programmatic change? a combination of the above? You may find that this kind of planning takes a semester or year to complete, but it is critical to the long-term success of WAC and well worth the effort (as the directors of the various programs described in this book will attest).

Program Goals and Workshop Format. Workshops are a vehicle for changing faculty perceptions about writing and learning and thus changing classroom practices and curricula, but change takes time. We recommend selecting the length and format of the initial WAC workshop in light of your broad program goals and with the expectation that you will plan additional and ongoing workshops. One popular format for a first workshop is an introductory program for faculty who need information about WAC before they elect to participate in longer, more intensive sessions. This scenario often includes an outside consultant/presenter who delivers a morning address to all faculty and then leads a hands-on session for those who want to know more. Longer workshops or a series of workshops are planned as follow-up. In this model, the first workshop generates interest in WAC and introduces participants to basic WAC concepts.

If there are already initiatives similar to WAC on your campus (such as critical literacy or computers across the curriculum), the first workshop can be an intensive one (four days or more) for 15 or 20 faculty. The goal might be that each participant redesign a syllabus to integrate writing into one of his or her courses. Follow-up meetings provide opportunities for participants to discuss how the changes are progressing. Another way to begin is with a series of half-day workshops spread over an academic year. Participants form a working group to learn about writing across the curriculum and to discuss their experiments with writing assignments. Members of the working group become excellent candidates for a collegewide writing council or WAC committee.

Fortunately, WAC workshops now have a track record as a proven means of faculty development, and information on various models is available in several of the sources listed at the end of this chapter (see especially Fulwiler and Young; Stanley and Ambron; Peterson).

The Planning Group. An early decision in planning the first workshop is the makeup of the planning group. If your school has a WAC committee or writing council in place, they are a natural choice. If not, a cross-disciplinary group that is representative of the audience for the workshop often works well. A small group with a designated leader who has released time may function more efficiently than a larger group working on the consensus model. On the other hand, spending a semester or a year planning the first workshop allows group members to educate themselves about WAC and even to develop into potential workshop presenters.

Audience. Gathering information about what the prospective audience wants and needs from a WAC workshop is an important responsibility of the planning group. How much do faculty on your campus know about current writing theory and research? How much do they know about collaborative learning, critical thinking, writing to learn, responding to student texts? Are they especially receptive to empirical research, to theory, to pedagogical applications? What are the power relationships among those in the potential workshop audience (i.e., will it include tenured and untenured faculty, full-time and adjunct faculty, administrators and staff as well as faculty)? Will you invite the entire faculty or only those from one discipline? Considering the audience early in the planning process allows you to coordinate its goals with those of the WAC program.

Topics. Topics at writing workshops develop naturally from two interrelated sources: the need for faculty to understand writing more fully and the concerns faculty have about using writing in their courses. Because both issues must be addressed to establish a sound and continuing WAC program, it is fortunate that they automatically give rise to subjects that are well suited to a workshop treatment. From the need for a better understanding of the complexities of writing come sessions about:

- Research in composition and rhetoric
- Writing to learn through informal assignments
- Learning to write through sequenced, formal assignments
- Understanding one's own writing processes
- Writing and authority
- Faculty writing groups
- Computers and writing
- Reading and writing
- Thinking and writing
- The rhetoric of specific disciplines
- Local research projects

From faculty concerns about assigning and responding to writing come sessions on:

- Planning, presenting, and sequencing assignments
- Expanding the assignment repertoire
- Responding to student writing
- Handling the paper load: quick methods, checklists, holistic grading, primary-trait scoring
- Helping teaching assistants to help students with writing
- Using computers for editing, revising, networking, electronic mail (E-mail) journals
- Establishing "standards": grammar, spelling, formats
- Using writing with nonnative speakers
- Coordinating with the English composition program
- Coordinating with the writing center
- Connecting reading, thinking, speaking and writing

These lists are not complete, and many of these topics are difficult to deal with quickly, yet they are inherent in the expanded use of writing that is the real meaning of writing across the curriculum. You will find additional ideas for topics in Tables 3.1 and 3.2, which contain sample agendas of two-day and five-day workshops.

Presenters. Obviously the person who leads a workshop is a major factor in its success. A first consideration is whether an outside consultant should be invited, whether an inside presenter would be better received, or whether a combination would be most effective. For whatever reasons, outside consultants are often assumed to have more expertise. Generally, their experiences at several campuses prepare them to handle such glitches as participants who want to assign blame (to the English department, to students, to the writing center) and participants who want to control the workshop. You may wish to hire an outside consultant for your first few workshops and then, as more faculty become knowledgeable, use internal talent. Some institutions hire an outside consultant to give a keynote speech at a full-day or several-day program, and ask their own faculty to lead breakout sessions.

TABLE 3.1. Sample Workshop Syllabus for a 1½-Day Workshop:
Assignments That Teach Disciplines

Day 1	
8:30-9:00	Coffee and pastries
9:00-10:20	General Session: Why WAC is needed and how it evolved over the years
10:30-11:45	Select one of the following sessions:
	A. Writing as a method of developing thinking and improving learning skills
	B. The question of precision in writing: Structural and grammatical precision as well as correctness in punctuation and spelling
12:00-1:30	Lunch
1:30-2:45	Sessions A and B above will be repeated
3:00-4:15	Select one of the following sessions:
	C. Matters of evaluation and grading
	D. WAC resources: articles, books, software
Day 2	
8:30-9:00	Coffee and pastries
9:00-10:15	Select one of the following sessions:
	E. Assignments that teach the Arts and Humanities
	F. Assignments that teach the Sciences
10:30-11:45	Divisional meetings assisted by the presenters
12:00-1:00	Closing Session: directions for the future; curriculum reform; applications of WAC elsewhere

NOTE: Designed by faculty at Monroe College, Rochester, New York.

A second consideration is the credibility a consultant or presenter will have at your institution. Research universities, four-year colleges, and community colleges have special characteristics that affect their writing across the curriculum programs. A presenter from the same type of institution will be more knowledgeable about mission, faculty loads, admissions policies, and publication pressures than a presenter from a different sort of institution. Presenters also have different styles. Some tend to begin with the history and principles of WAC; others start by asking participants to write first and then reflect on the experience. You might compare Anne Herrington's

TABLE 3.2. Workshop Syllabus for a Five-Day Workshop

Day 1 (Wednesday)
  1. Writing across the curriculum: the concept, the history
  2. The goals of the workshop (design at least two assignments, plan for implementation, evaluation)
  3. How we use writing in our lives
  4. The problems of student writers
  5. Present use of writing in your classes: what do you want to change?
  6. Informal writing
Day 2 (Thursday)
  1. Informal writing (continued): journal writing
  2. Tailoring assignments to course objectives
  3. Defining conceptual tasks
Day 3 (Friday)
  1. Informal writing assignment due: 11 copies
  2. Writing for different purposes and audiences
  3. Sequencing assignments
Day 4 (Tuesday)
  1. Formal assignment due: 11 copies
  2. Implementing assignments
      a. Staging assignments to facilitate the writing process
      b. Peer review
      c. The writing fellows program
Day 5 (Wednesday)
  1. Evaluating and responding to student papers
  2. The role of the library
  3. Revisions of assignments due

NOTE: Designed for faculty at La Salle University, Philadelphia.

article, "Writing to Learn" with Toby Fulwiler's "Showing Not Telling" for descriptions of different approaches. Of course, the best presenters use a combination of approaches and are sensitive to the audience's needs at different times during the workshop. Two good ways to select a presenter who will be credible on your campus are to attend workshops he or she leads on other campuses and to ask for recommendations from other WAC directors.

If you plan to present a workshop yourself, you will find useful advice in Toby Fulwiler's article, "Writing Workshops and the Mechanics of Change" and in Roy Fox's "A Saga of Unsung Symbols: Writing Assignments Across the Disciplines." These articles discuss how to design and lead a workshop that is filled with opportunities to write and reflect on writing. One of the best workshop writing prompts we know of is used by Susan McLeod who asks participants the following question: "What makes a good teacher in your discipline?" And a fine account of how to pace a workshop can be found in Weiss and Peich's article "Faculty Attitude Change in a Cross-Disciplinary Writing Workshop."

Funding. Workshop expenses may include some or all of the following: consultants' fees and travel allowances, stipends for participants, room rental, refreshments, publicity, mailing, administrative and secretarial support, photocopying, and incidentals. Having participated in a range of workshops from brown-bag lunches with volunteer, in-house presenters to summer institutes with lodging, meals, and honoraria, we know workshops can be effective regardless of budget. Nevertheless, our advice is to work hard for funding from all possible sources (grants of all types, presidential or provost funds, professional development budgets, departmental budgets, alumni or college foundation monies, corporate or business resources). Once funding levels are set, look at the workshop budget from several angles. Can you schedule a well-financed, initial workshop if you follow it up with inexpensive sessions? Can you finance a nationally known consultant if he or she presents on your campus rather than at an off-campus retreat site? Can professional development credits for a weekly WAC seminar replace a stipend or released time? Can the culinary arts department provide refreshments at cost?

Consultants' fees will be a major portion of the workshop budget. Experienced presenters typically charge between $500 and $1,500 (plus travel expenses) for a one-day workshop. If the fees of a particular consultant exceed your budget, ask that person to recommend other consultants who live in your geographical area (to reduce travel expenses). The National Writing Project site in your state, neighboring schools with established WAC programs, and regional consortia are good sources for names of local presenters.

Nearby institutions might try co-sponsoring a workshop or scheduling workshops in the same week to share consulting fees.

The cost for an internal presenter can vary as well—from an
honorarium to a letter of commendation to a notice in an evaluation to all of the above. The main point is to select a person who
will be an effective workshop facilitator and then make every
effort to stretch resources to finance his or her fees.

Stipends for faculty participants are another budget item. Some
WAC programs provide money; others released time. Some provide meals and overnight accommodations if the workshop is
off-campus. Some give participants faculty guidebooks such as
Moss and Holder's *Improving Student Writing,* Walvoord's *Helping
Students Write Well,* or Tchudi's *Teaching Writing in the Content
Area.* A contrasting approach is occasionally used. Some institutions charge a registration fee to offset expenses (or in certain
cases, to guarantee attendance). The guiding wisdom here is either
to pay people (whether a stipend or a lunch) or to charge them as
an incentive to attend.

Costs for room rental, refreshments, publicity, photocopying,
administrative and secretarial support, and incidentals will vary
but should be included in your funding estimates. Robert Simerly's
recent book *Planning and Marketing Conferences and Workshops* contains a useful chapter on developing accurate and realistic workshop budgets. Simerly includes sample spreadsheets, budget forms,
and a budget checklist (80-101). Another important source on
WAC funding is Keith Tandy's chapter in *Strengthening Programs
for Writing Across the Curriculum.*

Scheduling. In most cases, the academic calendar dictates the
dates for WAC workshops. Perhaps the best times are the days just
prior to or just following the semester or quarter. Summer institutes are popular if the budget includes faculty stipends. Be sure
to coordinate scheduling with the professional development committee on your campus. This committee can work with you on
funding and publicity as well.

Publicity. Accurate, appealing, and extensive publicity plays a
major role in workshop success. We advocate the rule of three—
publicizing workshops a *minimum* of three times. For example,

you might distribute a flyer to all faculty, write an article for the faculty newsletter, and have WAC committee members make announcements at department meetings. Phone calls and personal notes to colleagues are always worth the effort. We recommend designing a WAC logo and displaying it prominently on WAC notices. Use the expertise of the marketing, art, or graphics professors on your planning committee. Include the name of a contact person and a phone number on all publicity.

Workshop Evaluations. Changes in pedagogical beliefs or in classroom attitudes are not easy to measure, yet workshop evaluations are vital for ongoing WAC programs. Consider using an evaluation that will serve as a planning tool for the next workshop—perhaps a set of open-ended questions, a listing of pluses and minuses, or a freewrite about classroom applications that the participant expects to try after the workshop. Margot Soven from La Salle University has used the following evaluation prompt with good results:

Dear Colleagues:

We appreciate your participation in our workshop. Please comment on the overall value of the workshop, and if possible, on the program for each day. Thank you for taking the time to share your impressions with us.

An alternative is a series of questions such as the following:

1. What were some strengths of the workshop?
2. What were some weaknesses?
3. Was the workshop what you had expected? Please explain.
4. Please comment on the ideas presented at the workshop.
5. Please comment on the presenters.
6. Would you recommend a similar workshop to a colleague? Why?
7. What might you like offered in a future WAC workshop?
8. Additional comments:

The evaluation form can be distributed and collected toward the end of the workshop with the provision that those who wish to write extensive comments may return the form through campus mail.

Other Considerations. When you hire consultants and make room and meal arrangements, you are entering into legal agreements. Check with the administration about standard contract forms for such things and find out who needs to review (and/or sign) the contracts you negotiate. Table 3.3 shows a sample consulting contract.

A week or two before the workshop, the planning group needs to double-check room and catering arrangements. This is the time to send out maps and parking stickers if they are necessary. On the day of the workshop, the planning group can welcome participants and make introductions. Someone should be responsible for last-minute errands such as photocopying. Someone should keep the presenters aware of the time so that the workshop moves at a good pace and includes an adequate number of breaks. *How to Organize and Lead a Faculty Development Workshop* by Mayo-Wells, Daston, and Keesing contains generic checklists that cover advanced planning and the workshop itself.

Other considerations are a written agenda, name tags, evaluation forms, paper, pencils, overhead projector, transparencies, chalk, and eraser. A display table with handouts, pamphlets, books, and bibliographies on writing is a fine idea. After WAC is established, this table provides space for contributions from participants—successful assignments, student papers, faculty writing. You might also coordinate a book display with the college's bookstore or library.

Follow-Up. Because WAC workshops are components of larger programs and because they are not one-time events, the planning group has important follow-up responsibilities. Thank-you notes (and checks) go to presenters. Faculty participants and those who provided funding or other resources should be thanked (and you can enclose a recent article on WAC or a flyer announcing the next session with your note). A brief report with a summary of evaluation comments will keep the faculty senate and the administration informed. A longer report with suggestions for the next workshop can be presented to the writing council or WAC committee. Articles in the WAC newsletter and in other publications smooth the way for future workshops.

TABLE 3.3. Sample Consultant Agreement Form

The signatures below constitute an agreement between

_____(name of institution)_____   and   ___(name of consultant)___

for   ___(name of consultant)___   to present a faculty workshop

about   _____(title of workshop)_____   on

___(date)___ from _____ a.m. to _____ p.m. at

___(location)_____   .   The honorarium for the

workshop is $_____ plus $_____ for travel expenses

for a total of $_____ .

Director, Writing Across the Curriculum   (date)

Dean of Instruction   (date)

(name of consultant)   (date)

Social Security Number or EIN
(Fed. Emp. ID No.)

- -

To be completed after the workshop:

Verification of Performance

Approval for Payment (Dean of Business Affairs)

SUSTAINING THE WORKSHOP COMPONENT

Once the initial WAC workshop has been evaluated and the WAC committee has decided to make workshops an ongoing part of the program, there are a few things to keep in mind. The mechanics of workshop planning remain the same, but the audience will now include veterans as well as newcomers to WAC. Some schools such as Oakton Community College in Illinois and La Salle in Philadelphia offer a multistrand approach for these audiences—repeating the introductory workshop and inviting veterans of that series to advanced workshops. Oakton's publication, *The Critical Literacy Project,* contains syllabi from their first-, second-, and third-generation workshops. Other schools such as Weber State in Ogden, Utah, invite uninitiated faculty to the first part of a workshop and have veterans join newcomers during the last part of the session. At Prince George's Community College and at Montgomery College, where one-day workshops are often topic specific, we welcome veterans and newcomers alike on the assumption that each will contribute to and take from the workshop what he or she wants.

Some Friendly Advice. Whether planning a first or fifth workshop, here are some things to keep in mind:

- Workshop attendance should be voluntary. As Melissa Kort reminds us, faculty are "for better or worse, adult learners," accustomed to autonomy (21). If you require advanced registration or a fee, it's a good idea to be flexible about last-minute additions as long as space is available.
- Don't assume that faculty will understand writing to learn or will redesign their assignments after one or two short workshops. Attending a workshop is easy; actually changing assignments or classroom dynamics is hard. Extensive workshop time and follow-up resources are critical for faculty trying to integrate writing into their courses. Support may take many forms such as one-on-one consulting (see Kuriloff, this volume), a WAC newsletter, a faculty writing group (McLeod and Emery), and a cross-disciplinary writing center for students (see Harris, this volume).
- Avoid planning too much for one workshop or too many workshops for one semester.
- Don't give up if one workshop bombs. An unsuccessful workshop is a learning experience, not the end of a program.

CONCLUSION

WAC workshops are not one-time events. If faculty development is an integral part of your WAC program, you will find that workshops become integral as well. Over several semesters, you may offer sessions for different constituencies: faculty, teaching assistants, administrators, students. Workshop cycles can be repeated or can be incremental. Workshops provide time for participants to study writing theory, write for themselves and others, collaborate with colleagues, redesign their classes and assignments, and reflect on language and learning. Workshops build interdisciplinary connections and lead to additional program components: curricular changes, peer-tutoring, writing centers, classroom research, and collaborative teaching. Workshops that foster faculty dialogue, model WAC values, encourage reflexive pedagogy, and demonstrate the connections between research, theory, and classroom practice are invaluable components of WAC programs.

WORKS CITED

The Critical Literacy Project. Oakton Community College, 1600 East Golf Road, Des Plaines, IL 60016-1268.

Fox, Roy F. "A Saga of Unsung Symbols: Writing Assignments Across the Disciplines." *Journal of Teaching Writing* 5 (Spring 1986): 133-50.

Fulwiler, Toby. "Showing, Not Telling, at a Writing Workshop." *College English* 43 (Jan. 1981): 55-63.

———. "Writing Workshops and the Mechanics of Change." *Writing Program Administration* 12 (Spring 1989): 7-20.

Fulwiler, Toby, and Art Young, eds. *Programs That Work: Models and Methods for Writing Across the Curriculum*. Portsmouth, NH: Boynton, 1990.

Herrington, Anne J. "Writing to Learn: Writing Across the Disciplines." *College English* 48 (Apr. 1981): 379-87.

Kort, Melissa S. "No More Band-Aids: Adult Learning and Faculty Development." *ADE Bulletin* 95 (Spring 1990): 21-24.

Mayo-Wells, Barbara, Melissa Daston, and Hugo Keesing. *How to Organize and Lead a Faculty Development Workshop or Seminar*. College Park, MD: Faculty Development Program, Undergraduate Dean's Office, University of Maryland University College, 1982.

McLeod, Susan H., and Laura Emery. "When Faculty Write: A Workshop for Colleagues." *College Composition and Communication* 39 (Feb. 1988): 65-67.

Moss, Andrew, and Carol Holder. *Improving Student Writing: A Guidebook for Faculty in All Disciplines.* Dubuque, IA: Kendall-Hunt, 1988.

Petersen, Bruce T. "Additional Resources in the Practice of Writing Across the Disciplines." *Teaching Writing in All Disciplines.* Ed. C. W. Griffin. San Francisco: Jossey-Bass, 1982. 75-82.

Simerly, Robert G. *Planning and Marketing Conferences and Workshops: Tips, Tools, and Techniques.* San Francisco: Jossey-Bass, 1990.

Soven, Margot. Mimeographed handout.

Stanley, Linda C., and Joanna Ambron, eds. *Writing Across the Curriculum in Community Colleges.* San Francisco: Jossey-Bass, 1991.

Tandy, Keith A. "Continuing Funding, Coping With Less." Strengthening Programs for Writing Across the Curriculum. Ed. Susan H. McLeod. San Francisco: Jossey-Bass, 1988. 55-60.

Tchudi, Stephen N. *Teaching Writing in the Content Areas: College Level.* Washington, DC: National Education Association, 1986.

Walvoord, Barbara F. *Helping Students Write Well: A Guide for Teachers in All Disciplines.* 2nd ed. New York: MLA, 1986.

Weiss, Robert, and Michael Peich. "Faculty Attitude Change in a Cross-Disciplinary Writing Workshop." *College Composition and Communication* 33 (Feb. 1980): 33-41.

FOUR

Starting a WAC Program

Strategies for Administrators

KAREN WILEY SANDLER

As administrators become more concerned about student writing, it is natural for them to turn to the literature for assistance. Unfortunately, little guidance is available for the administrator struggling with questions about writing programs and how they can best be sustained on the individual campus. While much has been written (and continues to be written) about what WAC is, how successful programs work, and how WAC techniques change student learning, the administrator faced with the challenge of implementing and supporting a fledgling program is frequently on her own. As a French-teacher-turned-administrator, I bring a special dual perspective to the challenge of beginning and maintaining effective WAC programs, and—not unlike any other aspect of academic administration—that challenge yields more readily when I first turn to my faculty instincts for guidance.

Those instincts and my experience provide some simple advice: Keep in mind that your role is to support and encourage good curricular activity on your campus. As other contributors to this volume have noted, it is impossible for an administrator, no matter how knowledgeable in WAC theory or practice, to construct a top-down writing program. You must, therefore, look for co-conspirators and work with them to design a WAC program with the right fit for your campus.

THE FACULTY DEVELOPMENT WORKSHOP

My experience as a faculty member invited to participate in a WAC seminar is probably not dissimilar from that of many colleagues. The invitation came to me at lunch while I was enjoying some leisure time with our campus' new director of writing, Toby Fulwiler. When Toby suggested that I participate in the writing workshop he was planning for faculty from all sectors of the university, I felt a slight twinge of annoyance. Here was a new colleague inviting me to learn about writing without appearing to exhibit the slightest comprehension of the fact that—as a French language teacher—I taught writing all the time. However, the invitation was offered with such a spirit of sharing and collegiality that I decided to attend the workshop and see what happened next. I also decided that the workshop might give me the opportunity to let my colleagues in English know what kind of writing training foreign language students received.

The workshop itself put my annoyance far behind me. Toby's approach was to ask each participant to reflect on his or her own classroom experience and to bring to bear on that experience the insights we were gaining together at the workshop. I was excited and encouraged to discover that the kinds of writing I had been assigning—presumably in isolation—was the subject of careful discussion and positive interest. Journal writing, freewriting, collaborative activities, my other attempts to free students from their fear of playing with language were brought into a theoretical and practical focus that gave me new ideas and new encouragement. I left the workshop feeling validated in my pedagogy and intrigued to find out more, to continue the conversation about writing. Today, having participated in, organized, and led various WAC workshops, I wonder at Toby's ability to keep the missionary zeal out of sight, to offer that workshop as an opportunity for successful practitioners of the art of teaching to validate each other's experience. Essential to that successful workshop was the attitude Toby has repeated many times in print: "that's really what a writing workshop is—a time and a place for sharing among teachers who care" (Fulwiler 63). In short, successful WAC directors draw from the strengths of each faculty member they contact;

they depend on and grow with their colleagues as they work together to build a program that will change attitudes (and pedagogy) relating to writing.

AFTER THE WORKSHOP:
CONTINUING THE CONVERSATION

My experience as a faculty member leads me to this central observation: Working with faculty from many disciplines is likely to be the most challenging and the most intellectually exciting part of building a WAC program. For example, following that first workshop, I was invited to join a group of faculty (who all happened to be in the English department) for weekly brown-bag sessions to talk about writing. Writing meant any writing: professional writing, your students' writing, pedagogical approaches to teaching writing, whatever. The only requirement was that you had to share regularly some experiment, research project, observation, or paper. What began to dawn on me as a member of a large faculty body was how isolated I had felt and how exciting it was to connect with colleagues with similar interests. I shared a paper I had been working on—with little success—for some time. The comments of the group helped me get it accepted for presentation. Others discussed classroom experiments; others shared drafts of journal articles. I hardly remembered feeling resentment against English department colleagues. Now I knew them; I was working with them and they, with me.

As a spin-off of that group, another group of faculty began to meet regularly. We were interested in ways to teach more critical thinking in our classes; we wanted to apply current cognitive theories to our teaching practice. Toby, as part of that group, kept writing central to the discussion. Gradually, my horizons were expanding; so were Toby's; so were the others'. I left the university shortly afterwards, but that group went on to sponsor summer workshops for teachers and to promote other changes in the curriculum. Connections abounded. New ways of viewing one's discipline and practice emerged from these conversations. New viewpoints kept challenging my definitions, methods, and expectations.

OPERATIONALIZING WAC ON YOUR CAMPUS

As I draw on my experience as a WAC faculty member, I am convinced that faculty commitment is the necessary (and sometimes sufficient) contributor to successful continuation of WAC on a campus. If you, as an administrator, wish to see WAC flourish on your campus, you must foster faculty interest and dedication; you must allow faculty to own the program, and build it, and customize it—bit by bit—to suit your curriculum. Like an expectant father, there is much you can do to help, but some things by the nature of your job will be beyond your capacity.

In my role as an academic administrator, I have worked on two campuses to strengthen WAC programs. On one campus, the commitment had already been made to establish such a program and a director of writing had been hired before I got there. On the second campus, several elements were already in place, but the understanding of what WAC really is and what it implies for teaching and learning rested almost exclusively in the mind of an overworked senior faculty member. The campuses were quite different in other respects, but in each case a writing center already existed (with released time available to the director), there was at least tacit commitment on the part of the college administration and faculty to improve student writing, and I was able to lend support in specific ways.

On the first campus, my supportive role focused on helping the nontenured faculty member advance WAC ideas despite resistance from her department chair. This took the form of persuading the provost to maintain her released time each year as her chair tried to assign her more sections to teach, sharing tasks with her (such as all the organizational details for the writing workshops), putting her in touch with faculty who would be interested in WAC and who could be influential with others, and helping her in obtain internal and external grants for her own research. You might say that I was a behind-the-scenes hand holder and cheering section. I took every opportunity to find her time, allies, and money while she established the program.

However, on the second campus, I happen to be the administrator most directly responsible for supporting a WAC program. This situation presents an interesting dilemma, one that I share with other academic administrators who are knowledgeable about writing theory: I am charged with the well-being of the program and know more about running it than most on our campus, but I cannot (and should not) lead it. The following are some observations derived from my experience, ones that can be applied not only to WAC but to any desired curricular change (see Sandler "An Administrator's View"; Glick).

1. Never try to start a program by yourself. If you actually manage to get something going despite the normal resistance faculty feel toward administratively launched curricular initiatives, the program will not last. Faculty know how to design courses and teach. Administrators know how to provide support and design structures to keep good ideas alive. Keep the lines separate and let each group do what it does best.

2. Exert all the influence you can in the hiring process. If you ever need to be interventionist, it is in this aspect of establishing the program. If you are directly involved in the hiring process, look carefully at each curriculum vitae for clues about the candidate's attitude toward writing, use of writing in her own teaching, and actual knowledge of writing theory (this latter is vital if the hire is to be in the English department). Ask your writing director and/or those most knowledgeable about writing to screen credentials with you and to help you design interview questions that will give you a good read on the candidate's potential as part of a WAC program. If you are not the hiring authority, try to get faculty associated with WAC to serve on search committees and work to get questions on writing included in the interview process. Hiring of new faculty is one of the most important areas for shaping the campus climate; depending on who you select, you can get to the critical mass needed to sustain a WAC program more quickly than you may have imagined.

3. Find the best teachers on campus and get them interested in WAC concepts. The two campuses where I have supported WAC programs already had talented and respected faculty members interested in developing a program. However, I am convinced that the concepts associated with WAC are those that would excite the interest and enthusiasm of any talented classroom teacher. If I, as an administrator, were to start a program from scratch, I would seek out imaginative and innovative teachers (one or two would suffice) and send them to conferences where they could learn something about WAC. The First Year Experience conferences (sponsored by the University of South Carolina) work well for this purpose, as do national assessment conferences such as the American Association

of Higher Education's Assessment Forum. (Incidentally, the AAHE also published an excellent collection of essays about WAC that can help inform both faculty and other administrators; see Smith et al.) In addition, there are meetings of the National Network of WAC Programs every year at the National Council of Teachers of English Conference (NCTE) and the Conference on College Composition and Communication (CCCC), mentioned in Chapter 2 of this book. Without directly trying to impose my ideas on these faculty, I would take the time to have lunch with them, talk about what I know about WAC, refer them to some basic books and articles, and/or put them in touch with some knowledgeable WAC faculty at nearby institutions. The concept of using a "lead teacher" to gather a critical mass of enthusiastic and interested faculty is a tried-and-true method to bring about important curricular change.

4. Do not depend overmuch on the English department for these lead teachers. Although you can expect your English department faculty to have the training in writing theory and to have had far more experience in teaching writing, you should be aware of the talent available among other faculty on your campus. There are, for example, your colleagues in the foreign language department who also teach courses in composition. They may already employ some of the same successful WAC techniques you want other faculty to learn (for some examples of this kind of cross-over, see Sandler "Letting"). Some of the most imaginative writing assignments I've seen have originated in the History departments at small colleges. At my institution, a junior colleague in geology (who has never participated in a WAC seminar, although I keep trying to get him to come) uses writing to learn as if he knew these techniques instinctively. Collaborative learning techniques are frequently features of courses in schools of business, education, and agriculture. Oral communications faculty members use many ungraded informal writing assignments to encourage critical thinking in their students. The most successful WAC program will be that one that draws on the strengths of all participants, that brings people together to solve teaching problems together, and that highlights what already works in others' classes.

5. Once you've found your lead teachers, give them the support they need. If your budget is sufficient, help them find off-campus workshop consultants or send them for training. Give them some money to purchase books, go to conferences, join organizations, or visit nearby campuses. If you have a limited budget, make some of those unpleasant choices and find them some modest support money. I believe that money spent on a good faculty workshop (with hono-

raria for participants if possible) and a well-run writing center is your best use of funds (see Harris, this volume). I would rather do a few things slowly than rush the process. Let the quality of WAC concepts sell the idea for you; do fewer activities, if you must, but do them extremely well.

6. I'm fond of faculty writing workshops as a way to elicit interest, but I have never billed these workshops as a way to improve faculty writing or faculty teaching of writing. Rather, I have focused on these workshops as my way of supporting improved teaching. The workshops I've sponsored have always been optional, although I will talk to faculty about why I think they might enjoy the workshop if I have a good working relationship with the faculty member. I have often convinced someone to attend by confessing that I felt that person's viewpoint was critical to the intellectual respectability of the workshop or by telling an outstanding teacher that I needed excellent teachers at the workshop to give the ideas a fair trial. Do not try to screen out people whose views you think might be disruptive, although you should always inform your workshop consultant of the potential audience (see Walvoord, this volume). Workshop consultants should come to you with a great deal of experience at handling various group dynamics, and you should check with references before engaging any consultant to be sure he or she can handle resistant faculty. There is no quicker way to kill professional interest than to try to stack the cards in favor of your preferred teaching philosophy. Invite your best teachers no matter what you think their attitude toward WAC will be. They will probably surprise you anyway.

7. Recognize your faculty's interests in pedagogy and in research. Faculty will participate in a writing workshop because they have some interest in solving classroom problems or in improving their students' reasoning abilities. However, they are all practitioners who have professional interests beyond the classroom. Help to bring out the research areas related to writing, especially those that would be relevant and useful on your campus. For example, can someone document a relationship between certain writing assignments and improved test scores or improved performance in a course? What writing assignments are more appealing to a specific learning style? Is there a qualitative difference in classroom discussions when certain writing assignments precede those discussion? If you can use some faculty development funding to encourage your best researchers to work on these questions, you strengthen several components of campus life at the same time. What originally attracted me to WAC

was the potential to improve my students' learning. What has kept me engaged continually is the opportunity to develop intellectually.

8. Make connections, encourage connections, nourish connections. The intellectual attraction of WAC programs lies in their peripheral advantages as well as in their central mission. At small colleges as well as larger research institutions, faculty work with a sense of isolation and alienation that is counterproductive. You and your faculty will have to learn a great deal about other disciplines to recognize what writing approaches will be most useful (and what approaches won't work). Develop a network of interested faculty and then depend on them for advice. If you are demonstratively willing to learn from your colleagues, if you are a thoughtful listener, if you will provide the administrative support without working from the top down to establish a program, you will succeed where a "missionary" will fail. You may also find your faculty making unforeseen connections in productive collaborative efforts (see, for example, Soven and Morocco; Fulwiler and Strauss; Soven and Simon).

9. Link WAC concepts to improved teaching rather than improved writing. If possible, play down the idea that with the help of a WAC program students will finally learn to spell. Some faculty harbor real fears about their own writing and they will quickly (and erroneously) come to the conclusion that a writing workshop aimed at improving student writing will expose them to professional embarrassment. Needless to say, exposure to writing-to-learn philosophy as well as learning-to-write concepts frequently has a liberating effect on these faculty, but they won't get exposed to these ideas unless you can get them to attend. One of the best teachers on my campus almost skipped a WAC workshop (which she eventually attended and loved) because she felt so negative about her own writing. I was able to convince her to attend by citing some of the instructional aspects the workshop would address, aspects she was very interested in developing. Then there are those faculty members who take great delight in red inking every student paper while telling anyone who cares to listen about how poorly students write these days. You don't want them to attend a workshop with the expectation that they are going to learn more about paragraphing and spelling. The workshop leader will have a difficult enough time convincing people like this to try process writing techniques; don't compound the problem by false advertising. WAC programs take on a life of their own only by having a positive and lasting effect on teaching.

10. Provide as many rewards as you can for those involved in WAC. It is particularly important to reward your lead people. Released time for your WAC director is crucial. Conference travel money, a book

budget, and a celebratory lunch or dinner for participants and friends of WAC are all possibilities. Keep your eyes open to unexpected sources of income; try to find interested donors, grant money, and other resources. It's essential to let people know that WAC is a proven, sound, and cost-effective means of improving instruction; as such, it becomes an institutional priority. If you don't have money, find less expensive ways to say thank you. Write follow-up memoranda expressing your appreciation for the impact WAC lead teachers are having on the curriculum (with copies to their department chair, their personnel file, and the dean or president). I once used a small budget available to me to invite a faculty member to take two favorite students to lunch as a way of saying thank you. If you are in a position to influence (or to make) tenure and promotion decisions, let it be known that WAC involvement is a positive step. Remember that at some times during the establishment of a WAC program, your lead teachers may feel embattled, isolated, or underappreciated. You have to work to give them a sense of your commitment, which will carry them (and you) through any hard times.

11. Let your support of WAC be widely known, but do not appear to espouse a party line. Always approach the WAC issues in the spirit of instructional innovation and support. Your approach must say to all faculty, "I support this program because it works to improve teaching, but I'm always keeping an open mind about its components; let's try it and see what happens." No matter how much you think you know about various approaches to teaching writing, let your faculty lead. You'll learn more that way and your campus's WAC program will be its own.

12. Be patient and let the program build on its own quality. You will need to contain your desire for quick conversions. You cannot rush excellence; it grows and ripens only with time, integrity, and care.

13. Don't neglect your established faculty. Frequently, an administrator will believe that newer faculty are more supportive of curricular change. This is not necessarily true, especially on a campus that values teaching above other faculty contributions. As you look for lead teachers, pay close attention to the award winners or ask students to tell you who are the best among the experienced faculty. A few lunch conversations talking about teaching may then offer you the opportunity to share what you know about writing. However, offer just enough to elicit interest. Your experienced faculty cohort can give you perspectives that add stability to and understanding of the campus culture to balance the energy and innovation of the newcomers (a group that may include yourself). Trust them and depend on them as much as they permit.

14. Make it pleasant for faculty to continue the conversation after the first workshop. Faculty are busy; they frequently feel pressured with little (perceived) support from the administration. As you encourage their interest in WAC, you will need to be mindful of the stresses of their lives. WAC should alleviate, not add to, that stress. I always try to provide a relaxing and pleasant physical environment for the writing workshops; this includes providing, if possible, for really good food.

You can be quite creative about continuing that faculty conversation. Borrowing an idea from the University of Vermont's Writing Program faculty, I instituted at one campus what I called a Faculty Wretreat (*Writing* + *Retreat*). This was billed to faculty as a time to get away from campus to a pleasant and quiet environment where they would not be interrupted and where all needs would be met for them while they used the time to write anything they wanted. (One person wrote a computer program!) We provided a large room with partitions, computers and word-processing programs, snacks, restrooms, outdoor lounge furniture (it was at a ski resort in May), some tables for group work, and three meals a day. We also provided overnight accommodations for those who wished. The Wretreat lasted two days, during which time faculty wrote when and as they wished. It was a tremendous success for the 15 people who attended. What it accomplished was to encourage some conversation about collaboration, some sharing of manuscripts for peer editing, and (unplanned as it was) conversation over lunch about the positive effects of the WAC workshops on classroom situations. Because half the participants had not yet attended a WAC workshop, this latter event was much welcomed.

YOU ARE NOT ALONE

Recalling the success of the Wretreat for both WAC-ed and non-WAC-ed faculty brings me full circle. The value of a writing across the curriculum program lies in its effectiveness in connecting faculty in all disciplines with each other for continuing and meaningful conversation about teaching. The writing program on any campus consists of teachers sharing with teachers. Remember this, and you can overcome many obstacles. Forget it, and you lose momentum.

The more you rely on your teacherly instincts, the more successful and permanent will be your WAC program.

When the academic administrator confronts the task of initiating and supporting a WAC program on campus, the first impression could easily be that it will be a lonely task. From my experience, I want to assure you that this impression is probably wrong. The results of my involvement in the WAC program on the campus where I served as a faculty member can be summarized in two words: validation and connection. After almost 10 years of involvement in supporting WAC programs, I still come back to those two words. The administrator can find renewed energy and inspiration through active listening to faculty colleagues who can lead the way. Working with WAC as an administrator will offer unique opportunities to reconnect with faculty colleagues and to reconfirm the essential commitment to teaching, which serves us all—faculty and administrators—as the common and changeless bond.

WORKS CITED

Fulwiler, Toby. "Showing, Not Telling, at a Writing Workshop."*College English* 43 (Jan. 1981): 55-63.

Fulwiler, Toby, and Michael Strauss. "Interactive Writing and the Teaching of Chemistry." *Journal of College Science Teaching* 16 (Feb. 1987): 256-62.

———. "Writing to Learn in Large Lecture Classes." *Journal of College Science Teaching* 19 (Dec. 1989): 158-62.

Glick, Milton D. "Writing Across the Curriculum: A Dean's Perspective." *WPA: Writing Program Administration* 11 (Spring 1988): 53-57.

Sandler, Karen Wiley. "An Administrator's View of the Old Chinese Curse: We Do Live in 'Interesting Times.' " *Toward a More Inclusive Curriculum: The Integration of Gender, Race, and Class.* Gaithersburg, MD: Ephemera, 1989: 89-92.

———. "Letting Them Write When They Can't Even Talk? Writing as Discovery in the Foreign Language Classroom." *The Journal Book.* Ed. Toby Fulwiler. Portsmouth, NH: Boynton, 1987: 312-20.

Smith, Barbara Leigh, et al. *Writing Across the Curriculum.* Current Issues in Higher Education 3. Washington, DC: American Association for Higher Education, 1983-84.

Soven, Margot, and Glenn Morocco. "Writing Across the Curriculum in the Foreign Language Class: Developing a New Pedagogy." *Hispania* 73 (Sept. 1990): 845-49.

Soven, Margot, and Barbara Levy Simon. "The Teaching of Writing in Social Work Education: A Pressing Priority for the 1990s." *Journal of Teaching in Social Work* 3 (1989): 47-63.

FIVE

Writing Across the Curriculum and/in the Freshman English Program

LINDA H. PETERSON

Creating a writing across the curriculum course for—or WAC component of—the English department seems like a contradiction in terms. The writing across the curriculum movement has had as one of its major goals the dispersal of writing throughout undergraduate education. That goal has been formulated for diverse reasons, some practical (e.g., that the English department cannot assume sole responsibility for teaching writing or that writing skills learned in freshman English need reinforcement), others theoretical (e.g., that writing is a mode of learning or that undergraduate education ought to introduce students to conventions of thinking and writing in various disciplines). Whatever the reasons, writing across the curriculum programs have advocated a movement beyond—indeed, away from—the English department.

Nonetheless, the freshman English course can provide a major component of a comprehensive writing program and, if well conceived, can become the basis for subsequent writing across the curriculum efforts (see Hilgers and Marsella, ch. 7). The practical reality, at many institutions, is that freshman English is the one required course in writing, one that all students hold in common. What freshman English requires often defines for students what "writing" is. If freshman English is a course that asks students to read literary texts and write about them, then it represents "writing" as training in literary criticism. If freshman English instead asks students to read and write contemporary prose forms (the autobiographical essay, the character sketch, the cultural critique, and so on), then it provides an introduction to nonfictional writing. If, however, freshman English asks students to read and write in various academic genres, then it may provide a foundation for writing in the disciplines. This preparation is important for all undergraduates who plan advanced work in their majors and, later, in their professions; it is even more important for less well prepared students who need a general introduction to the features of academic discourse (see Bartholomae).

Obviously, a director of writing across the curriculum cannot mandate that the English department offer this third sort of course. As Barbara Walvoord suggests in Chapter 2, writing directors and administrative officers should never force a program or curriculum onto any faculty. Departments believe, quite rightly, that the courses they offer must fit into a coherent set of offerings. And if the freshman course is to be taught primarily by members of the English department, then it makes sense for the approach to be compatible with the department's sense of its methodology as well as with the writing across the curriculum program's sense of its mission. In English departments that take a broad view of English studies—a view that includes linguistic, rhetorical, and textual studies—a freshman course focusing on forms of academic prose may be possible, even desirable as part of its undergraduate sequence.

THINKING THEORETICALLY, CONCEPTUALIZING THE PROGRAM

The model outlined in the following pages aims for both conceptual compatibility and administrative practicability. It is, according to Susan McLeod's distinction in Chapter 1, a *rhetorical,* or *learning-to-write,* model. It begins by drawing on an essential technique of English studies: rhetorical analysis of the ways that conventions operate in forms of written discourse. This model does not assume that English faculty can or must master the complex subject matters and methodologies of disciplines other

than their own. It does assume, however, that English faculty
teach rhetorical analysis as fundamental to their discipline: that
they regularly show students how conventions operate in literary
texts, how those conventions both enable and limit the writer, how
they make reading possible and pleasurable for the reader. As
Jonathan Culler puts it in *Structuralist Poetics*, we cannot read a
literary text, certainly not "interpret" it, without competence in
the conventions of its genre: Readers bring to the work "an implicit understanding of the operations of literary discourse which
tells [them] what to look for" (113-14).

Similarly, readers and writers of "nonliterary" texts—whether
a quantitative report by an anthropologist or a descriptive analysis by an art historian—need to understand the conventions. The
concept of *convention*—literally a "coming together," a shared
understanding about matters of structure, style, evidence, and
theme—is as important in a writing class as it is in a literature
seminar. Student writers, whom thinkers like Elaine Maimon have
characterized as apprentices in a field, need to understand the
conventions of thinking and writing in that field. The concept of
convention, if not the term itself, is crucial to the student's success
in undergraduate courses.

Consider, for example, the knowledge required of a biology
student assigned a laboratory report in its standard form. The
student needs to know the conventional structure: title, abstract,
introduction, materials and methods, results, discussion, and references. She needs to understand conventional distinctions among the
sections: that, for example, the "results" section presents the facts
discovered in the past tense and in both statistical and verbal
forms, whereas the "discussion" section interprets the facts in the
present tense, explaining their significance and relation to other
work in the field. And she needs to understand the conventions
of scientific style, what might be called an *effaced style*, if one refers
to a deemphasis of the experimenter, or a *highlighted style*, if one
refers to an emphasis on key objects and facts.

Such conventions of the lab report may, at first glance, seem a
far cry from the conventions of an English sonnet or a classical
epic. Yet the English teacher's means of understanding these
forms, like his or her way of teaching "close reading," derive from
techniques of rhetorical analysis. A freshman course within a
writing across the curriculum program might focus on learning

such techniques and applying them to a broad range of academic discourse. Traditionally, English teachers have taught students to recognize conventions and to explore the use to which writers have put them in the creation of literary texts. In a writing across the curriculum program, English teachers might transfer this knowledge of convention and its enabling power to forms of writing that are not strictly literary: to historical essays, psychological case studies, reviews of anthropological literature, and scientific lab reports.

This transference can represent the English department's contribution to the writing across the curriculum program (or part of it). The goal of freshman English, at the most basic level, would be to teach students how to recognize and use central conventions of writing in the disciplines by applying techniques of rhetorical analysis. This goal would link the students' desire to take a *practical* course with the English faculty's desire to show how rhetorical analysis, a central aspect of its discipline, complements other parts of a university education. Beyond this basic goal, the course might engage students in the process by which conventions are created and established. It might show students how conventions are shaped by an agreement between writers and readers in a shared field of discourse, and it might demonstrate, via faculty dialogue, how these agreements are constantly being renegotiated as fields expand and change.

The rationale for adopting this model might be articulated as follows: Professionals within a discipline share a knowledge of the conventions of written discourse used by that discipline. Such knowledge needs to be shared with students, too. English faculty can, with the help of others, encourage this sharing by introducing students to the written work of professionals in various disciplines, by showing them how to read that work for conventions as well as content, and then by asking students to try their hands at apprentice versions of such writing.

TURNING THEORY INTO PRACTICE

The writing director who wishes to design a freshman course that focuses on forms of academic writing needs to begin by consulting faculty in several different departments. To repeat

Barbara Walvoord's advice, "Start with faculty dialogue" (this volume). When members of our freshman English staff decided to try this approach, we contacted colleagues in five fields: art history, history, biology, anthropology, and philosophy. The exact fields are not crucial, but a representation from the humanities, social sciences, and natural sciences provides an important mix of discourse styles. So, too, cooperative colleagues from those departments are important—not because they must team teach the writing course, but because they must provide substantial advice and assistance.

We asked for the following advice: (1) What are some examples of good writing in your field? (2) What are typical assignments that a freshman or sophomore might encounter in your department? (3) What tips would you give students for writing successfully in your field?[1]

With such information, a freshman staff can design a course with four to six units, each introducing students to writing in an area of academic study. In a typical unit, students would read examples of exemplary writing in the discipline; would try, with the help of the writing instructor, to identify central conventions of this writing; would do a typical assignment, ideally an apprentice version of the professional form; and would have an opportunity to ask questions of (or hear advice from) a faculty member in the discipline. Other sound pedagogical techniques from *cognitive models* of writing across the curriculum—such as using heuristics, keeping journals, writing drafts, and eliciting peer commentary—would be incorporated into each unit. We regularly used peer workshops, for example, to help our students generate ideas and revise drafts during the course of each unit.

In planning the course, the writing staff might consider the following principles and procedures.

1. Working with colleagues to choose examples of good writing may be more productive than searching through professional journals or relying on collections of essays. On their own, English faculty may choose writing they perceive as exemplary, but it is not necessarily writing admired by professionals in the field. Colleagues in other departments can suggest well-written, representative, even humorous articles that the English teacher would never find independently. They can also recommend a wide range of texts that demonstrate the various strategies used by scholars in their discipline.

Given the increasing number of textbooks on writing across the curriculum, it is possible, of course, to shorten this process of collecting exemplary writing. Textbook authors and editors, some of whom are contributors to this volume, have already done the hard work of assembling and then testing materials for classroom use. But even if a staff decides to adopt a writing across the curriculum textbook, it would be unwise, I think, to sidestep entirely the process of soliciting examples of good writing from one's colleagues. Faculty benefit immensely from the conversations that develop as they discuss good writing with each other. Students benefit from discussing writing that a professor at their home institution has chosen, perhaps even written. There is no pedagogical substitute for talking with a professor about how she or he wrote an article, what procedures she or he used, and how much trouble she or he had.

2. Asking colleagues for advice in formulating assignments can strengthen the link between the freshman writing course and the broader college curriculum. In my experience, colleagues will readily share paper topics from their introductory courses or help writing faculty invent topics modeled on actual assignments from introductory courses. The assignments the students do in freshman English will directly relate, therefore, to the writing they do throughout the university.

Sometimes colleagues even suggest examples of professional writing that provide instant paper topics. An anthropologist from Union College, for example, contributed two versions of an essay he had co-authored: one for a professional journal, *Current Anthropology*, the other for a popular magazine, *Psychology Today* (see Gmelch and Felson; Felson and Gmelch). Not only did these essays demonstrate how writers adapt materials for different audiences but the professional version actually included a survey that students could repeat to generate data for their own writing assignment. The survey—on forms of "magic" used by modern college students—had only to be reproduced and distributed to a new population. Thus the professional reading naturally produced the students' research and writing: Students became apprentice anthropologists as they added new data to, and tested the theoretical statements in, the work of a professional anthropologist.

3. Inviting colleagues to join in a class discussion, to respond in person to questions about academic writing and its conventions,

can aid the writing program's efforts to show the differences and similarities among the disciplines. Such discussions give students a chance to ask questions that they normally cannot—or will not—ask in large introductory courses. (Not coincidentally, they remind professors of issues that should be raised regularly, even in "content" courses.) When I teach such a course, students use these informal discussions with professors to ask questions that, although central to a discipline, are rarely if ever raised in other contexts: "What is an historical fact?" "What does it mean that writing in the sciences is 'objective'?" "Why do literature teachers tell us not to refer to the 'author' or his 'message'?" These questions can aid the goals of the general education or core curriculum programs at many liberal arts institutions.

English faculty could, of course, teach an introductory writing across the curriculum course without asking colleagues to lead a discussion or respond to students' questions. But a colleague's presence lends authority to the approach. It shows how professionals within a field use conventions as part of their working vocabulary and as means for generating ideas. Discussions also demonstrate how collegial relationships work. We—English faculty as well as students—felt free to raise issues about academic writing that we knew we could answer only partially but that we expected to be able to resolve with the help of an additional perspective.

4. Using class time for collaborative work keeps the focus on the students' writing and on the kinship between professional writers and apprentices in the field (see Bruffee "Structure of Knowledge"). It is tempting to devote class time primarily to analyzing professional texts and questioning guest professors about strategies for success in their disciplines. As in all writing courses, however, the focus should stay on the students' own work. To make this possible, writing teachers should encourage collaboration among peers. Collaborative workshops give students a chance to practice methods of invention or strategies of revision and to define for themselves the modes of argumentation and presentation that delineate the conventions of a discipline.

Certain writing assignments can encourage this collaborative methodology further. For instance, a biologist now teaching at the University of Virginia, Nancy Knowlton, suggested that students conduct pseudoexperiments that would allow them to focus on the form of the scientific report, rather than on an actual research problem. (They did Coke versus Pepsi tests, experiments with homemade versus "refrigerator" cookies, taste tests of various foreign foods.) Knowlton also suggested that students work in teams, just as they might in a research lab. As the students gathered data and later as they wrote up their findings, they worked collaboratively, dividing up the research and writing tasks. Such division reflects the actual procedures of professional scientists, who seldom write every section of a research report on their own but instead rely on teamwork to produce research and writing.

ANTICIPATING THE DIFFICULTIES, AVOIDING THE PITFALLS

Introducing writing in the disciplines, by using these principles and procedures, helps to address a pedagogical problem that often surfaces in freshman English. When students write within an academic setting, they often try to compose what they think the teacher wants. Often, too, they approach successful writing as the arbitrary result of the luck—or bad luck—they had when they got assigned to an individual composition teacher. Teaching convention helps us redefine these (false) premises by shifting focus away from the individual teacher and toward the academic discipline: They as student writers are expected to recognize and apply a core of conventions agreed on by an academic community (see Bruffee "Structure of Knowledge"). What we as writing teachers do is redefined as helping students learn to discover and master such conventions.

Although a freshman course in academic writing may resolve this pedagogical problem, it may not help writing programs (or program directors) avoid more fundamental conceptual and administrative problems. Two problems tend to originate within the English department, three others outside of English.

English departments that define themselves narrowly (or perhaps, in fairness, I should say specifically) as departments of literature may be unsympathetic to a freshman course that focuses on "nonliterary" reading and writing. Especially if English departments have been pressured into service, into teaching every incoming student in a required writing seminar, they may not wish to add to their burden by teaching materials unfamiliar to them. The freshman course I have described works best in an English department that defines itself broadly as a department of language and literature, that places rhetorical issues at the center of English studies, that takes an interest in nonfictional prose forms, that sees itself as interdisciplinary, and that assumes a wide definition of what is "literary" or even rejects the distinction between the literary and nonliterary. This sort of English department will find teaching writing in the disciplines challenging and intrinsically interesting.

If a writing director does not have a sympathetic English department with which to work, it may be better to accept a different model for the freshman course. A more traditional course that uses various prose forms—some literary, some academic, some popular genres of nonfiction—can still provide an appropriate introduction to composition, so long as it incorporates sound pedagogical practices from "cognitive" models of writing across the curriculum. An introductory course in literary criticism may be an appropriate contribution for the English department to make to the writing across the curriculum program—if it is (re)conceived as a course that teaches not just literary texts, but the conventions of reading and writing about literary texts. (This approach has been adopted, for example, at SUNY Albany.)

A second problem may also originate with the English department, although it may have little to do with antagonism or incompatibility. This problem surfaces when the primary instructors for freshman English are graduate students in English, but the primary instruction they receive as graduate students is in literary history and criticism. To teach an introductory course in academic writing, an instructor must have some familiarity with nonfictional prose forms, some understanding of the rhetorical techniques and issues at stake. Many students beginning graduate study have no experience with nonfictional prose—let alone with rhetorical strategies for analyzing forms of academic prose. Many have never taken freshmen English themselves; some have avoided, as undergraduates, exposure to disciplines other than English. As a result, they may find teaching a writing across the curriculum course more difficult than freshmen, with a broad range of interests and backgrounds, find taking it.

To avoid this pitfall, the graduate program should include course work not only in composition theory and pedagogy but also in forms of nonfictional prose. It is possible to compensate for a lack of such courses by devising a strong teaching practicum—one that addresses issues in academic writing, perhaps one that invites faculty from across the university to discuss professional writing with graduate teaching assistants (TAs). But assistance at the graduate level cannot be ignored—without disastrous effects on the freshman course. Whether formally through course work or informally through workshops, novice instructors will need help teaching a writing across the curriculum course. (This point holds true at colleges where regular faculty comprise the writing staff, but because faculty have more experience as teachers, the difficulties can be solved quite readily with a strong faculty development program.)

Not all difficulties involve the English department. Some derive from the practices that this model of teaching writing across the curriculum assumes. For instance, when colleagues suggest examples of good writing, they may in fact select writing that is inappropriate for use with freshman students: it may be too difficult, it may pursue an intellectual problem too abstruse, it may contain passages of "bad writing" (even by the standards of the professor who has chosen it). These less-than-ideal choices can cause difficulties in the classroom. They need not cause disasters, however. In conversation with writing instructors, faculty will often admit that a piece of writing is difficult for freshmen, but that they assign it anyway to illustrate essential techniques of academic writing. Or, in discussions with students, faculty will acknowledge that an exemplary article contains passages of dull or poor writing, but that overall it represents powerful strategies of argumentation.

Admissions like these can lead to crucial discussions about standards for academic writing. Students can come to understand how a piece of writing may be both "good" and "bad," how and why writing may be "powerful" at certain moments but "dull" at others, how writing may be "acceptable" in its use of conventions but "poor" writing nonetheless. And, because students have the opportunity to study multiple forms of academic writing, they can begin to formulate differences in disciplinary standards. In a discussion with a biologist, for example, one student asked why the scientific report had so few transitions—a feature that history and literature professors emphasized as essential. The biologist was able to explain that sections of the scientific report must stand on their own, without verbal transitions; further, she explained that the logic of paragraphs within sections must be clear without a reliance on transitional devices.

In other words, difficulties with suggested readings can become occasions for significant learning in the classroom. As the writing program develops and English faculty gain experience, some writing suggested by colleagues may be "disappeared" or replaced by other selections. Some freshman staffs may decide, too, that they will concentrate only on writing about a discipline or writing done by professionals for a lay audience. These choices may be necessary, but in my experience, the ideal version of the freshman writing across the curriculum course uses real academic writing, in combination with these other forms of prose. In most instances the difficulties that academic essays introduce can be turned into pedagogical assets.

This is less true for difficulties with suggested writing assignments. Colleagues in other fields sometimes propose assignments that cannot be completed without a course in the department or at least some understanding of the subject matter. A history paper we initially assigned asked for a comparison of different positions taken during the Civil War on the meaning of the Preamble to the Constitution ("We the people of the United States..."). The rhetorical techniques needed for analyzing the documents and writing the paper were relatively simple (the compare/contrast paper is, after all, one of the most common assignments in postsecondary education). But the historical background needed to complete the paper proved a stumbling block to foreign students. American students enter college with basic information about the American Civil War, whereas foreign students do not. The assignment put the latter at a disadvantage.

By quickly adding background reading and by encouraging collaboration, we were able to compensate for our initial blindness to the difficulties of the assignment—and we avoided the problem the next time around. Yet every assignment in a writing across the curriculum course has the potential, in some way, to put some student(s) at a disadvantage. The biology major will find writing a scientific report easier than a prelaw student will; the humanities major will probably prefer writing about a literary text or an art object to writing up a psychological case study. Although this reflects the reality of a liberal arts education, writing instructors can avoid the pitfall of unnecessarily privileging or disadvantaging certain students by thinking through the skills needed to complete an assignment and then by evaluating assignments at the end of the course.

And this point raises the last—and most knotty—problem: that, even with careful planning and evaluation, this model for writing across the curriculum may be too difficult for some freshmen at some institutions. Both David Bartholomae and Patricia Bizzell have written about incoming college students for whom the general practices of academic discourse are unfamiliar and intimidating. For these students, a more general introduction to academic thinking and writing may be preferable—with this more discipline-specific model saved for a second-semester or junior-level course. Only the individual writing program director, familiar with students at his or her home institution, can decide the case. But I might point out that variations on this freshman English course have been tried successfully at institutions as diverse as Carleton and Beaver Colleges, UCLA and Utah State, and the University of Pennsylvania and Yale.

Despite potential difficulties, a freshman-level introduction to academic writing can provide a sound basis for a writing across the curriculum program. The course can challenge English faculty to apply their expertise as scholars and critics to written texts not traditionally included in the literary canon. It can help TAs in English see the broad application of the rhetorical strategies and generic conventions they are studying at the graduate level. And, most important, it can help incoming undergraduates comprehend the modes of thinking and writing that underlie the courses they are—and will be—taking.

NOTE

1. For a detailed description of how an individual unit in such a course might work, see Moore and Peterson. I wish to thank Leslie Moore for her years of collegial friendship and for her permission to rework ideas developed together in teaching freshman English.

WORKS CITED

Bartholomae, David. "Inventing the University." *When a Writer Can't Write.* Ed. Mike Rose. New York: Guilford, 1985. 134-65.

Bizzell, Patricia. "College Composition: Initiation Into the Academic Community." *Curriculum Inquiry* 12.2 (1982): 191-207.

Bruffee, Kenneth A. "Collaborative Learning and the 'Conversation of Mankind.' " *College English* 46 (1984): 635-52.

————. "The Structure of Knowledge and the Future of Liberal Education." *Liberal Education* 67 (1981): 177-86.

Culler, Jonathan. *Structuralist Poetics: Structuralism, Linguistics, and the Study of Literature.* London: Routledge, 1975.

Felson, Richard B., and George Gmelch. "Uncertainty and the Uses of Magic." *Current Anthropology* 20 (Sept. 1979): 587-88.

Gmelch, George, and Richard Felson. "Can a Lucky Charm Get You Through Organic Chemistry?" *Psychology Today* Dec. 1980: 75-77.

Hilgers, Thomas L., and Joy Marsella. *Making Your Writing Program Work: A Guide to Good Practices.* Newbury Park, CA: Sage, 1992.

Maimon, Elaine. "Talking to Strangers." *College Composition and Communication* 30 (1979): 364-69.

Moore, Leslie, and Linda Peterson. "Convention as Transition: Linking the Composition Course to the College Curriculum." *College Composition and Communication* 37 (1986): 466-77.

SIX

Writing-Intensive Courses
Tools for Curricular Change

CHRISTINE FARRIS
RAYMOND SMITH

While many writing across the curriculum programs began as quick-fix projects the mission of which was the overall improvement of student writing, the programs that have managed to become permanent fixtures are likely to be those that have moved from "writing crisis" management in the direction of curricular change springing from faculty experimentation with a variety of uses of writing. The original WAC vision (e.g., different components of the unified liberal arts curriculum using writing to solve similar "tough problems") is complemented at some institutions by a growing local knowledge of how thinking, reading, and writing are different under different disciplinary and pedagogical conditions.

RATIONALE FOR WRITING-INTENSIVE COURSES

Ask most of the founding mothers and fathers of WAC programs just what ideas sparked the program at their institution and they are likely to give you two answers: (1) students' writing skills will diminish if not reinforced and practiced between freshman composition and graduation and (2) students' writing improves most markedly if they write while they are engaged by their major subject. The WAC program at the University of Missouri-Columbia, for example, is predicated on the notion that freshman composition courses cannot do the whole job of improving student writing, while La Salle University's Writing Emphasis Course guidelines stress that "professionals in the field (instructors) should evaluate advanced writing in the major since they are more familiar than faculty in the English department with the content and stylistic conventions of writing in their fields." (Margot Soven: unpublished handout) These two notions are hardly irreconcilable—some universities demand general education writing-intensive courses as well as a capstone writing-intensive course.

But the WAC programs that have had the most durable (and in our view most felicitous) effect on curricula owe those efforts to yet another premise held by faculty practitioners: writing disrupts the conventional lecture/test/lecture pattern almost ineluctably associated with large research-based universities. Especially in WAC's more recent history, the mainspring of many programs has become the intent to improve on what Freire calls the "banking model" of education in which students passively receive, record, and return the teacher's deposits of knowledge. Guided by work in cognition and critical thinking (Bloom; Perry), some faculty recognize writing-intensive (WI) designations not as an administrative obligation to demand the requisite number of pages and revisions but as opportunities to encourage in their students intellectual abilities that cannot be engendered through conventional courses.

The cognitivist perspective, of course, is not the only one that informs practice and shapes WAC programs. Programs like Georgetown University's, which include in their mission a "rhetorical" awareness of writing *within* disciplines, not just *across* disciplines, hope that students will achieve an understanding of "the relationship between writing (the writing in the assigned texts and the writing prepared by students) and what it means to become members of that discipline's intellectual community" (Slevin et al. 13). This concomitant cultivation of students' awareness of disciplinary ways of knowing, their critical thinking, and their writing abilities represents, quite obviously, a real change in the curriculum, especially at large research universities. In brief, pedagogy informed by the WAC movement has galvanized curricular change when the use that is made of writing has intellectual and social consequences for both students and instructors. However, if WI courses are to endure as more than a prefix in a catalog, faculty need to retain full ownership of the changes that come about after they attend workshops, consult with WAC program staff, and incorporate writing in their courses.

DEVELOPING WRITING-INTENSIVE COURSES IN THE DISCIPLINES

Faculty ownership of writing-intensive courses is often difficult to reconcile with the administrative mandates, requirements, and criteria that often permit large-scale WAC programs to prosper. But, as Susan McLeod has pointed out, some central administrative setup is needed to monitor and nurture genuine curricular changes ("Writing" 342). In making the decision to require a course with a substantial amount of writing beyond freshman composition, schools are faced with either placing greater demands on the English department to teach advanced writing courses emphasizing various disciplines or involving all departments in the teaching of writing. If the latter route is taken, a number of policy questions need to be resolved: Who will determine criteria for WI courses? Who will approve courses as fulfilling the WI requirement? In anticipation of the demand for courses that will fulfill the WI requirement, guidelines need to be developed that strike a balance between rubber stamping any course with a required term paper and an insistence on criteria, workload, or pedagogy too restrictive for some faculty members.

What Makes a Course "Writing-Intensive"?

Guidelines for WI courses at different institutions are strikingly similar; most include at least some of the following elements or something like them.

1. *Class size or instructor/student ratio.* Most guidelines insist that WI classes include no more than 15 to 25 students. In programs with

larger classes, teaching assistants may be provided to reduce the instructor's workload.

2. *Who teaches?* Many guidelines insist that WI courses be faculty taught rather than taught by teaching assistants (Indiana, Missouri, Michigan).

3. *Required number of papers or words.* Some guidelines indicate a total of, say, 5,000 words, which may include some combination of formal and informal writing, in-class and out-of-class writing, drafts, and journals, though guidelines may specify the number of formal papers (minimum of four at Indiana) or, like Missouri, that "2,000 words should be in polished papers."

4. *Revision.* Some guidelines specify how many papers should go through a complete revision process. Guidelines may indicate that drafts may be read by the instructor, peers, and teaching assistants or readers. Some guidelines make clear that feedback and revision must involve more than pointing out and correcting surface errors.

5. *How writing will affect final grade.* Guidelines may stipulate or recommend that grades on written work make up a certain percentage of the course grade. This is a point sometimes not easily negotiated in WI courses taught by disciplinary faculty. A total of 70% of the grade devoted to writing would be good; 20% is probably too low. At Indiana, students wishing to take a course for WI credit sign up for an adjoining course number and receive S (satisfactory) or F (fail) for the writing component of the course, which instructors are free to separate from the rest of the course.

6. *Types of assignments.* Guidelines may require or recommend that writing be spread throughout the course in a sequence of related assignments rather than concentrated in a large term paper. Guidelines may specify that a certain number of papers engage students in particular tasks, e.g., summary, analysis, integration of sources. Departments or individual instructors may be asked to generate assignments that discuss ethical issues of the discipline, or expose students to a disciplinary problem to be solved, or to a question on which experts disagree.

7. *Assignment-related instruction and evaluation of papers.* Guidelines may suggest, require, or provide teaching techniques demonstrated in workshops, for example, collaborative work, directed lessons on research techniques, checklists for feedback on drafts, and minimal marking.

8. *Support services.* Guidelines may suggest or require that WI course instructors make use of available consultation with the WAC staff, or that their students use the tutoring services in the campus writing center.

Role of the WAC Program in
the Development of WI Courses

On various campuses, WAC specialists and WAC programs play very different roles in the development and maintenance of WI courses. If a WI requirement is established apart from or prior to the creation of a WAC program, and courses meeting minimum specifications are designated "WI" by the administration or departments, WAC personnel may have the advantage of functioning independently (perhaps consulting with WI and non-WI course instructors alike), without the direct responsibility for incorporating writing in a hundred or so courses. At the University of Washington, for instance, a part-time WAC consultant is on the staff of the campuswide Center for Instructional Development and Research. If WAC staff have the opportunity to intervene during the creation of a WI course, they must ensure that faculty maintain final control over the shape of the course. While the WAC consultants may acquire expertise in how writing functions in, say, history or business, it is the faculty member teaching the course who should identify the disciplinary ways of knowing that writing might enhance or reflect.

To that end, writing specialists instrumental in initiating a WI requirement on their campuses may find themselves, willingly or unwillingly, eventually relinquishing or sharing authority over WI courses. When La Salle University began its WAC program, the Writing Emphasis Course Advisory Committee, appointed by the deans and composed of faculty representing different disciplines, was available to consult with departments who were responsible for developing courses according to the approved guidelines for the upper-division writing requirement. However, the committee had no formal authority to veto the department's choices. After the courses were developed, the advisory committee was dissolved, and the deans, in consultation with department chairs, assumed responsibility for periodic review of the upper-division writing requirement.

At SUNY-Albany, where a two-course WI requirement (one lower-division and one in the major) has replaced freshman composition, the writing center staff runs workshops and roundtable discussions and consults only when asked with faculty members who submit their WI course applications to the dean, not to a WAC committee or program. Departments are responsible for offering as many seats in approved WI courses as there are students majoring in the field.

At Indiana University, the intensive-writing requirement in the College of Arts and Sciences has been in place since 1980, when a collegewide committee recommended which already-existing courses in each department might incorporate a writing component. The Campuswide Writing Program, instituted in 1990, has no obligation to produce WI courses or to administer the requirement: Our mandate is to assist faculty in all schools and colleges within the university with their teaching of writing, not just those in arts and sciences. While we do not need to devote our energy to course generation and approval, what passes for intensive writing in some courses, is, as we say in the Midwest, "not our pig." We found, as did the writing center staff at SUNY-Albany, that writing-intensive guidelines, originally developed and passed by an administrative or legislative body on campus, typically say more about the WI requirement for students than they do about pedagogy conducive to writing.

Our experience tells us that writing does not necessarily go all the way across the curriculum. Not all departments feel obliged to offer WI courses, despite calls from administrators and other departments bearing most of the load. English departments, not surprisingly, often find themselves teaching the lion's share of WI courses; after all, chairs of other departments quite often maintain that "the English department has more experience teaching writing, and we cannot imagine how writing could be used within our courses."

FACULTY-CENTERED CONTROL OF
THE WRITING-INTENSIVE REQUIREMENT

To ensure that the concerns and conventions of disciplines across the entire campus are reflected not only in the original guidelines but also in how WI courses are monitored, some WAC programs manage to be essentially faculty driven by maintaining a permanent advisory committee that meets regularly with the support of WAC personnel. Courses that fulfill a WI requirement can be developed by individual faculty members with WAC program guidance and approved by the advisory committee made up of faculty from a variety of departments and colleges on campus.

At the University of Michigan, faculty members design their junior-senior WI courses and present them to the English Composition Board (ECB)—the writing center for the College of Literature, Science and the Arts (LS&A)—for review and approval. The ECB Policy Committee, made up of the ECB director, seven LS&A faculty and two ECB faculty, advises the ECB director on all matters related to writing at Michigan and reviews for approval all new WAC course proposals. Although most of the course descriptions submitted to them by faculty include a minimum of 30 pages of writing and emphasize revision and sequences of assignments, there are no central program guidelines for course approval (Hamp-Lyons and McKenna 258).

At the University of Missouri-Columbia, faculty also design their own WI courses following the Campus Writing Program guidelines and submit their applications to the program's Campus Writing Board, made up of faculty from all disciplines. Unlike some advisory committees, the role of which is to recommend courses for WI designation or to assist departments in doing so, the chief function of Missouri's board is the approval in disciplinary subcommittees (e.g., humanities, social sciences, and so on) of applications and reapplications. At Missouri, faculty must apply or reapply each semester to have their course designated WI; no course or instructor is anointed "WI" for life.

Applicants provide as much information as possible about their intentions or their past use of the writing component in their courses by attaching syllabi and examples of writing assignments. Committee members, knowledgeable about particular fields, courses, and reasonable disciplinary expectations for student writing, may suggest that guidelines be altered on an ad hoc basis when strict observations of the guidelines would do violence to the course. One of the Missouri guidelines, for example, suggests that "each WI course should include one paper that addresses a question on which reasonable people can disagree." Faculty in the natural and applied sciences pointed out that in some courses students were not yet able to question the central axioms of the discipline.

In a faculty-driven WAC model, the WAC director and program staff are able to function as "agents" of the approval committee rather than as missionaries, informing applicants of the committee's concerns and working closely with them on a WI course design that better meets program guidelines or disciplinary needs. The WI application and review/approval process, however, should not become a WAC program's raison d'être, replacing informal opportunities for the exchange of ideas among colleagues. Other pitfalls to avoid in the WI course approval process include the tendency to err in one of two directions: either to approve any course that comes down the pike in an effort to respond to the demands of a WI requirement or to make approval criteria so stiff that the committee in its zeal infringes on the academic freedom of colleagues or makes the curricular changes required by WI not worth faculty effort. Liz Hamp-Lyons acknowledges that "a loose hand on the reins of the curriculum is an essential corollary" of WAC at Michigan, for too many restrictions on the junior-senior WI course would make faculty at a research university less willing to teach those courses (Hamp-Lyons and McKenna 266).

Like Michigan's, Georgetown's WAC program considers one of its strengths to be its "commitment to the integrity and independence of individual faculty" (Slevin et al. 26). Program administrators there are generally confident that by making writing the central concern in a course, "instructors can only improve on what they do best." They admit, however, that one of WAC's major principles, "writing as a way of learning," has not especially caught on at Georgetown. They conclude that many of the faculty who incorporate writing do not view it cognitively but rather actively and rhetorically—as a response to prior writing, as persuasion in sociology, or an exchange among biologists. What follows from writing, they surmise, is more important to most faculty than what precedes it: the novice writer beginning to construct meaning and join that disciplinary dialogue that faculty value. Georgetown's efforts to rebalance the direction their WAC program has taken include follow-up discussions with WI faculty that emphasize how texts are produced in the discipline, especially how students struggle to produce their texts (27).

FACULTY INCENTIVES

Stipends. Faculty stipends are only one way to encourage faculty to volunteer to teach a WI course in programs where they have a choice. The English Composition Board at the University of Michigan awards both outstanding course proposals from faculty and contributions made by graduate teaching assistants. At the University of Massachusetts-Amherst, faculty receive additional salary for teaching a WI course. Workshops, of course, provide an excellent means of attracting prospective WI teachers and rewarding veterans. In addition to honoraria for first-time attendance at a workshop, WAC administrators might also consider honoraria ($200 to $400) for faculty attending their second workshop, for it is here, undistracted by the necessarily hortative nature of first workshops, that they will have the luxury to reflect on the exigencies of using writing in their courses. We recommend, by the way, that every workshop agenda include presentations by faculty who have taught WI courses. Local faculty, as opposed to itinerant WAC revivalists, speak with an authority that can seldom be matched. Money might also be set aside or procured from a university faculty development fund for summer stipends to faculty members who wish to spend time with WAC personnel seriously redesigning their WI course after teaching it for one term. In our experience, this has been money well spent.

Teaching Support. A big incentive for some faculty to teach a WI course can be teaching assistant (TA) or grader support provided by the WAC program to relieve the student paper workload. Georgetown University's Writing Program, for instance, provides TAs with special training in the teaching of writing so that even large lecture courses may be taught as WI, with TAs leading WI discussion sections. TAs meet in discipline-specific groups with WAC program staff to formulate methods for integrating writing, reading, and speaking experiences in the discussions and conferences for which they are responsible (Slevin et al. 17).

At the University of Missouri, quarter-time TA support is provided for every 20 students in a WI course after the first 20 (a course enrolling 40 students would receive, for example, one quarter-time TA, a course enrolling 60 would receive half-time support, and so on). The course application process requires the instructor to indicate how TAs and graders will be used, trained, and supervised. It may be necessary for WAC program personnel to monitor the TA/faculty work relationship at first to be sure that everyone's interests are best served. The WAC program director may wish to run (or be a significant participant in) the WI instructor's meetings and training sessions with TAs, to ensure that TAs are indeed responsible for tasks related to student writing (conferences, commentary on drafts, and supervised grading) and not shouldering all the WI burden. Consulting services offered by the WAC program to WI faculty can include "norming" sessions in which program staff guide the process by which a course instructor and TAs reach consensus on writing assignment goals and criteria.

The pitfall to avoid here would be a sort of mutual exploitation on the part of the WAC program, departments, and faculty: the creation of huge WI courses that fill the requirement, employ TAs, relieve faculty of extra work, but are not, because of their size, conducive to productive use of student writing. Large WI courses can be successful in every important respect (we have learned a great deal, for example, in working with an enviable 375-student WI journalism course). But faculty considering taking on such a task should keep in mind that their duties will become increasingly managerial. Our experience has been that critical mass for graduate student-assisted WI courses—that is, genuinely writing-intensive courses as defined above—would appear to be about 80 students.

Discipline-Specific Tutorial Services. The establishment of a writing laboratory or component of a writing center specifically for students enrolled in WI courses and staffed by tutors from the disciplines can be not only one of the key incentives for faculty involvement in the program but also one of the chief sources of data for the eventual improvement of how WI courses are developed and taught.

One important source of data for our consultation with faculty on the best use of writing in their courses comes from the course-specific tutors and the taping of tutor-student conferences on drafts. Because we see assignments and papers in flux, we have, through the operation of the laboratory, been given a view of the program we are administering perhaps unavailable to us through a more conventional program assessment scheme. Course-specific tutors who have worked with students grappling with the demands of assignments can tell instructors a great deal, for example, about the ambiguities of their assignments and the conceptual difficulties that those students encounter.

Reflection on Teaching Practice. It may seem odd to assert that the opportunity to reflect on one's pedagogy is a benefit of teaching WI courses; in fact, some instructors grumble that the struggle with the paper load makes reflection unlikely. WAC programs, however, often become something like a haven, particularly at universities where the gravitational pull of research is unremitting. Faculty development programs based merely on the exchange of "teaching tips" have little effect on individual pedagogies and, consequently, on the curriculum at large. A WAC program, on the other hand, can bring together faculty from disparate disciplines and modify teaching praxis, effecting, as one dean of our acquaintance has said, " 'subcutaneous' faculty development." At every university at which we have worked—and this has more to do with the nature of discovering writing as a tool for teaching than it has to do with our efficacy as consultants—WAC faculty participants have recognized that courses, like student papers, are in need of revision. And we should all know now what is meant by revision: not scrubbing away cosmetic difficulties, but rather examining the premises implicit in our pedagogies. Faculty willing to engage in this sort of reflection are the agents of curricular change at universities. These same faculty very often find their professional lives changed in meaningful ways—and for the better. They frequently win teaching awards for all the right reasons. WAC programs seem to breed the only tolerable form of elitism.

EVALUATING WI COURSES: HOW RESEARCH CAN INFORM PRACTICE AND CHANGE

For all the interest in the uses of writing in disciplinary courses, there has actually been relatively little formal inquiry into what happens in such courses once writing has been incorporated. Research on WAC often takes the form of investigation of the effectiveness of WAC on student learning (Applebee; Newell). The WAC movement seems to just now be reaching the stage where more formal studies are being directed at the various claims made for the value of writing in disciplinary classrooms. A growing number of ethnographies or case studies of how writing is taught in conjunction with how the subject matter is taught (Faigley and

Hansen; Herrington; North; Swanson-Owens; Walvoord and McCarthy) are taking into consideration important widespread differences as well as similarities across disciplines, courses, course levels, and perhaps most important, across students and instructors. To accomplish both the *cognitive* (writing to learn) and *rhetorical* (learning to write) goals of WAC programs, English-trained staff often find a need to place themselves inside the other academic disciplines, to learn about their subject matter, about their methods of study, and about what is valued in their writing. Without this immersion in other disciplines, WAC personnel run the risk of imposing their English-based perceptions on another field, perceptions that may not be all that conducive to producing WI courses that stimulate inquiry in disciplines other than their own. WAC consultants will find very quickly that they require more knowledge of the full context in which students' writing is produced and evaluated if they are to do more than help faculty reword assignments or make fewer red marks on papers.

One WAC assumption that often goes unexplored is that the dialogue Barbara Walvoord proposes will result in a transformation of pedagogy. Who knows whether two days of talk about WAC's cognitive and rhetorical aims will change the way faculty approach student writing the following semester? Some WAC programs have chosen to take their curiosity about follow-through or their anecdotal evidence of disciplinary differences in the way writing is used to a more formal level of inquiry, not as much for policing purposes as for what they will learn by looking at WAC *in practice.*

Consequently, more WAC programs are incorporating a "research arm" (SUNY-Albany, Illinois-Chicago, Indiana-Bloomington) to investigate how discipline faculty assign, respond to, and evaluate writing and how they put into play the texts of their discipline, the texts with which students must interact. The aim of such research is not to catch faculty who are not carrying out WAC guidelines but to learn ethnographically what their pedagogy means on their terms, so that together WAC programs and faculty can use writing to make courses better.

WAC faculty and staff at SUNY-Albany's writing center, for instance, have conducted case studies of several WI courses (North; Cain), some of the results of which were used in consultation with WI instructors. While that project was internally funded by the university, outside granting agencies like the Fund for the Improvement of Postsecondary Education (FIPSE) are still possible funding sources for WAC research. Internal funds set aside for assessment of departments and programs should not be overlooked. In the face of budget cuts, WAC programs that want to continue improving teaching and learning through writing may find they need to justify *how* they are accomplishing those aims. A proactive assessment of student writing performance in the full context in which that writing was assigned may head off the WAC program's forced participation in some form of standardized writing assessment mandated by administrators or legislators. Responsible attempts at assessment should after all make links between students' measured proficiencies and what has or has not happened to them in the full context of our courses and our classrooms, especially if, as we hope, assessment is to lead to reform in curriculum design. Contextual assessment can at the very least afford WAC programs and instructors opportunities to act together on their findings.

It was originally in response to a call for a standardized writing assessment of graduating seniors that we began investigating the disciplinary and classroom contexts in which WI courses are taught at University of Missouri-Columbia. A three-year study (Farris et al.) in collaboration with the WAC director and a professor in psychology enabled us to pursue questions we had as a result of tutoring sessions and interviews with WI instructors and, at the same time, interrogate one of the claims we and others have made for WAC—that it enables critical thinking. We combined ethnographic *thick description* of WI courses in journalism, art appreciation, and human and family development with two other lines of investigation, interviews with a sample of students before and after taking a WI course and those students' papers written in the course. Both the student interviews and the papers were rated on a scale of critical thinking derived from the work of William Perry and Karen Kitchener and Patricia King. Ethnographic thick description helped us determine why the level of critical thinking displayed in the writing was not consistent with the level students demonstrated in the oral interview.

We won't go into all our findings here, but just let us say that we are even more realistic WAC specialists for having done this research. We are able to say that the thinking students are able to engage in their writing for WI courses is contextually determined and includes assumptions of the discipline, belief systems of the instructors, and the extent to which those instructors have reflected on these in constructing class assignments and activities. We have a much better understanding of how WI instructor's classrooms really function as "interpretive communities." We have observed on a daily basis the extent to which both professional and student writing is integrated with course goals in the way it is shared, modeled, analyzed, and evaluated. More important, perhaps, we have a much fuller sense of what those goals mean to the members of that classroom's and that discipline's "culture."

For instance, for a number of years, a journalism professor's use of an assignment that called for the objective reporting of two sides of an issue conflicted with our sense that students in such a WI course should instead generate a committed position that drives their analysis of an unsettled issue. As a result of the semester we spent in this professor's classroom, we now understand more fully the place of that assignment in terms of his world view and the profession into which he believes he is initiating his students. We found reflected in all of his assignments, as well as in lecture and class discussion, the firm belief that, in a democratic society, journalism is responsible for the presentation of truth that emerges from a balanced consideration of viewpoints. We did suggest to this professor that his TAs hold one-on-one conferences for invention purposes, so that students, rather than choosing from a stock list of "point/counterpoint" topics (e.g., "Should the names of rape victims be revealed in the press?"), might at least explore an unresolved issue in journalism that was of particular interest to them.

Studying WI courses at close range can reveal that WI instructors do not always view the relationship between inquiry and writing in the ways we had imagined or in keeping with the WAC mission as it was first conceived. But research can give WAC personnel a better sense of WI instructors' epistemologies and provide data useful in consulting with faculty on the changes they want to make in WI courses. These are changes, that, finally, in keeping with or in spite of our "interpretation," integrate writing with what they would like students to be able to do in their courses, with their personal theories of the role writing plays in the construction of knowledge in their discipline.

A research and follow-up component can be the appropriate tack to take at what McLeod calls the *third stage* of WAC: in an effort to get beyond the implied success of the institutionalization of any idea—to a true investigation of how the program could remain interesting and effective ("Writing" 342). We believe that the way to keep writing tied to thinking and learning and to changes in teaching is to deal with it as locally and as discipline- and professor-specifically as possible. Such local work and co- investigation with faculty also deals most effectively with any fac- ulty resistance to "the colonizers." We strongly believe that the WAC programs that are most likely to last will be those that take their own advice on revision, those which are willing to continually re-see and adjust their claims, guidelines, and training materials in light of the instructor and student practices they encounter every day.

WORKS CITED

Applebee, A. N. *Writing in the Secondary School: English and the Content Areas.* Research Monograph No. 21. Urbana: NCTE, 1981.

Bloom, B. S., ed. *Taxonomy of Educational Objectives. Vol. 1: Cognitive Domain.* New York: McKay, 1956.

Cain, Mary Ann. "Researching Language Practices in Other Disciplines: Seeing Ourselves as 'Other.' " Conference on College Composition and Communica- tion. Boston, 1991.

Faigley, Lester, and Kristine Hansen. "Learning to Write in the Social Sciences." *College Composition and Communication* 36 (May 1985): 140-49.

Farris, Christine. "Trading Religion for Gold: Investigating Disciplinary Cultures and the Claims of Writing Across the Curriculum." In *Emerging Models of Language Cultural Studies.* Ed. Michael Vivion and James Berlin. Portsmouth, NH: Boynton, forthcoming.

Farris, Christine, Phillip Wood, Raymond Smith, and Douglas Hunt. *Final Report on Critical Thinking in Writing Intensive Courses.* University of Missouri-Columbia, Office of the Provost, 1990.

Freire, Paulo. *Pedagogy of the Oppressed.* New York: Herder, 1970.

Hamp-Lyons, Liz, and Eleanor McKenna. "The University of Michigan." *Programs That Work; Models and Methods for Writing Across the Curriculum.* Ed. Toby Fulwiler and Art Young. Portsmouth, NH: Boynton, 1990. 255-72.

Herrington, Anne J., "Writing in Academic Settings: A Study of the Contexts for Writing in Two College Chemical Engineering Courses." *Research in the Teach- ing of English* 19 (Dec. 1985): 331-61.

Kitchener, Karen S., Patricia M. King, Phillip K. Wood, and Mark L. Davison. "Sequentiality and Consistency in the Development of Reflective Judgment:

A Six-Year Longitudinal Study." *Journal of Applied Developmental Psychology* 10 (1987): 73-95.

McLeod, Susan H. "Writing Across the Curriculum: The Second Stage, and Beyond." *College Composition and Communication* 40 (Oct. 1989): 337-43.

Newell, George E. "Learning From Writing in Two Content Areas." *Research in the Teaching of English* 18 (Oct. 1984): 265-87.

North, Stephen M. "Writing in a Philosophy Class." *Research in the Teaching of English* 20 (Oct. 1986): 225-62.

Perry, William J., Jr. *Forms of Intellectual and Ethical Development in the College Years: A Scheme.* New York: Holt, 1970.

Slevin, James, et al. "Georgetown University." *Programs That Work: Models and Methods for Writing Across the Curriculum.* Ed. Toby Fulwiler and Art Young. Portsmouth, NH: Boynton, 1990. 9-28.

Swanson-Owens, Deborah. "Identifying Natural Sources of Resistance: A Case Study of Implementing Writing Across the Curriculum." *Research in the Teaching of English* 20 (Feb. 1986): 69-97.

Walvoord, Barbara, and Lucille P. McCarthy. *Thinking and Writing in College: A Naturalistic Study of Students in Four Disciplines.* Urbana: NCTE, 1991.

SEVEN

WAC and General Education Courses

CHRISTOPHER THAISS

TENDENCIES IN GENERAL EDUCATION COURSES

Doing WAC in general education courses has something in common with doing it in upper-level major courses—in both situations WAC can help people write better and learn better, and successful techniques that teachers use in their major courses can be adapted to general education. But adapt teachers must, because the differences between major courses and general education courses create big differences in WAC teaching and WAC program planning. Here are some key differences:

1. People do not major in general education, but are "forced" to take it. Prior motivation is low; resistance may be high.
2. General education courses tend to enroll freshmen and sophomores, people less comfortable and confident in the institution.
3. Especially in universities, class size tends to be larger, maybe much, much larger, than in major courses.
4. Courses are "introductory" or, in some programs, "interdisciplinary," so students lack knowledge of discourse and methods in the subject area of the course.
5. In four-year colleges and universities, faculty who teach general education tend to have less experience, less job security, and less

chance to communicate with other faculty than those who teach major courses.

6. The goals of general education courses tend to be vague and idealistic—e.g., "cultural literacy," "the ability to write in college," "appreciation of scientific method"—whereas goals of major courses tend to be specific and preprofessional.

7. Most general education requirements come in three- or six-hour chunks; there is neither continuity from one chunk to another nor any explicit connection between them.

Because of larger class sizes and because of relative lack of attention paid by full-time faculties to the general education courses in universities, examples of WAC programs focused on general education and core curricula are fewer than those of programs centered on the major, most commonly in writing-intensive courses. These tendencies create difficulties for WAC planners, but it is these tendencies that make writing so important a tool in general education. Writing can be the tool that helps us overcome the impersonality of large classes. It can help give confidence to the inexperienced, unsure new student. It can help students make connections between courses that seem arbitrarily chosen and isolated. Let me explore each tendency in turn and describe some WAC teaching techniques and faculty workshop practices that seem particularly relevant.

1. People Do not Major in General Education, but Are "Forced" to Take It. The most crucial thing to remember about general education is that people do not major in it. Faculties decide which subjects are essential toward producing a well-rounded individual and, therefore, require one or more courses in these areas. To varying degrees, choice is restricted. One school may have a large core curriculum of specific courses; another may follow the cafeteria model, wherein students choose from a list of courses within designated areas of the curriculum, for example, humanities, social sciences, natural sciences, and communication. Whatever the arrangement, someone besides the student is choosing what it is good for the student to know.

Hence, students often resist these courses. They treat general education requirements as something "to get out of the way" before the real work of the major. Moreover, even if a student is not hostile, the lack of choice implicit in general education require-ments means that the student is not likely to have thought much about the course before writing it into the schedule. So students enter the course having made no mental connections between it and anything of importance in life. Intrinsic motivation tends to be low.

If faculties genuinely believe in the usefulness of the general education requirements, then they need to find ways to (1) help students see the work as meaningful and (2) include definite choices that students can make within the course structure. Writ-ing can help bring about both objectives. For example, early in the semester teachers might ask students to write honestly and reflec-tively about the course: Why do they believe that this subject is required? How does it relate to other courses that are required? How does it relate to other things that interest them? How, do they suspect, might it be of use to them in the future? These writings can spark a class discussion, or at the very least clue the teacher in to issues to address in explaining and organizing the course.

In regard to choice, teachers can create writing assignments that allow students to exercise their individuality. Even in the course that rushes to cover a mass of prescribed material and tests stu-dents through standardized vehicles, it is possible to allow stu-dents to express themselves. Midterms and finals, for example, can include at least one essay question that asks for an application of knowledge to something else of interest to the student, or present a problem situation that allows real options. Better yet, teachers can give longer-term assignments that encourage an in-vestment of self and that reward uniqueness. If they want to spark outside reading, for example, they can let each student choose a text (do not require that all choices be made from a list you provide) and ask the student to write a review both for the teacher and for others in the class. Provide at least one class hour in which students can share their reviews with peers. Use the student choices to build a resource list to distribute to everyone.

In responding to student writing, teachers should keep in mind the need to stimulate motivation and make connections. Even a brief comment can specify attention to *this* writing by *this* student. Teachers should address students by name, comments should point out specific passages that interested the teacher, teachers should note connections that the writing sparked in them and perhaps suggest further sources for the writer to explore. Albeit concise, such a format expresses the teacher's enthusiasm for the subject and asserts the student's uniqueness.

2. General Education Courses Tend to Enroll Freshmen and Sophomores, People Less Comfortable and Confident in the Institution. Although a few colleges, such as Brooklyn College, have created core curricula that extend over four years, and although some schools such as the University of Maryland and George Mason have created upper-level required courses in writing, most colleges urge students to take general education course work early in their careers, so that the last two years can be devoted to the major. I realize, of course, that the increase in part-time students has made the "four-year" concept all but obsolete and that the lack of available sections in crowded schools has forced some students to put off general education courses until the last semester before graduation. Nevertheless, general education courses tend to enroll students either new or almost new to the institution.

Thus the general education course, regardless of the subject, serves as part of the student's "welcome" to the school. I put "welcome" in quotation marks because most institutions, particularly universities, devote to general education few regular full-time faculty and burden it with proportionately larger class sizes. Only recently, as drastic rates of attrition in the first year have generated concern, have schools begun to pay real attention to the quality of the welcome we provide new students, as witnessed by the rapid growth of the conferences on the freshman experience and by reports on general education from the Carnegie Foundation and the Association of American Colleges (Katz et al.).

How can WAC respond to the new student's need for welcome? If we take seriously the oft-reported values of writing in helping people explore their emotions, clarify their thinking, and establish relationships with others, then pertinent uses of writing come to mind, among them:

1. "Rapport" assignments
2. Constructive comments by teachers and peers on drafts
3. Electronic mail networks on and off campus

"*Rapport*" *Writing*. At the very least, writing should be suggested to faculty as a means for building rapport with new students. As an introductory exercise, teachers can ask students to introduce themselves: What are their interests and plans? What questions do they have about the course at this point? What strengths and weaknesses do they feel they have in relation to this subject? Even if they can't feel too comfortable writing about these things at the start of a course, at least the exercise will show that the teacher values their information and it gives the teacher the opportunity to respond with a word or two of welcome. Teachers of math and science frequently use assignments such as this as periodic checks of student morale during a tough course: What's problematic for you now? What do you have questions about? Math professor Stanley Zoltek of George Mason uses this technique as a standing assignment for an electronic journal that he uses to converse with his students via the computer (Thaiss et al.). Biologist Anne Nielsen of Blue Ridge Community College (Virginia) found that such invitations to students improved their morale and clued her in to student difficulties with concepts and vocabulary.

Faculty sometimes balk at the notion of encouraging students to write to them about such touchy-feely subjects as their personal relationships or their troubles adapting to college life. But as colleges and universities grow, and especially as they attract part-time and commuter students who are unlikely to use such campus services as counselors and dorm advisors, faculty of general education courses on occasion have to be willing to listen, lest their institutions lose many potentially successful students. This is not to say that writing in courses across the curriculum should be dominated by discussion of personal issues—far from it. Periodic checks of student morale are just that—maybe three times a semester. Within a required journal, for example, students can be assigned to write primarily about course concepts and data, but a few entries may be designated "free choice" or "anything you want to write about." Such entries may not even require a response, unless the student requests one; what's important is the opportunity to write.

Still, if students use such opportunities to write about issues that deeply trouble them, some thoughtful response is called for (Singer 72). Faculty often resist "how are you feeling?" assignments, because they fear the responsibility that accompanies the question and they recognize their lack of expertise in responding to emotional crises. For this reason, it is useful to invite to a faculty workshop a member of the counseling center staff to help the group discuss ways to be responsive to such writing without the teacher's having to take on the counselor's role.

Constructive Comments on Drafts of Papers. While feedback on drafts has become standard practice in courses devoted to the improvement of writing, we shouldn't overlook the importance of this practice in building rapport with students. Many teachers of composition find the one-on-one conference and the writing of helpful comments on drafts the most rewarding aspects of their teaching of writing, not only because of the growth this work occasions in student writing skill but also because of the sense of belonging that students derive from the personal attention. Later in this chapter I recommend that general education curricula be planned to include at least one course per semester in which students receive this kind of attention to their writing in progress.

This "rapport" role for feedback suggests again that teachers in their responses need to be sensitive to the writer as well as to the writing. We comment on and about papers, but we respond to people. In faculty workshops in WAC, it is essential to practice mutual responses to one another's writing and to stress that the same courtesy and thoughtfulness we grant one another needs to be granted students.

The need to show welcome through comments on drafts also points out the importance of the writing center on campus (see Harris, this volume). How many students come to the center initially on a teacher's referral to get help on a paper and then return to the center because of the genuine interest shown by the tutor!

In discussing feedback as instrumental both in the building of writing skill and in establishing rapport, I do not want to separate these motives. Indeed, this building of relationships through dialogue about writing is part and parcel of growth in writing, as I note later when discussing Tendency 4. When, for example, we ask students to elaborate points made in a draft of a critical paper or show how a draft of a laboratory report may be revised to fit classical form, we help initiate students to the language and conventions of disciplines, and so help them become better writers in those contexts.

Electronic Mail Networks. At more and more schools, local area networks (LAN) allow students to converse in writing with one another and their professors on topics as limitless as the imaginations of the writers. Students read all the contributions that have been made to the discussion and respond as motivated. Sometimes the conversations concern designated topics. As part of the computer literacy course in George Mason's Plan for Alternative General Education (PAGE) program, students receive access to BITNET and are assigned to read BITNET newsgroups. Each student chooses a newsgroup of interest to summarize and comment on to fellow students. This assignment promotes communication within special-interest groups and challenges students to describe their interests to those who know little or nothing about them.

3. Especially in Universities, Class Size Tends to Be Larger, Maybe Much, Much Larger Than in Major Courses. Although the National Council of Teachers of English (NCTE) has recommended 15 as the ideal size for the required composition class, and most schools keep this number below 25, few subject areas agree that general education can flourish only in small classes. While few try to defend the large lecture class as a forum for learning, large classes, of 50, 100, or several hundred, always look great on the balance sheet and many students abet this strategy by being satisfied just to find an open space. Full-time faculty go along because large classes for general education pay for small classes in the subjects they want to teach to majors and graduate students.

WAC program planners have found large classes to be stumbling blocks for their efforts in two ways. First, the teacher who tolerates the large lecture class as a suitable forum for learning has probably not thought deeply enough about his or her objectives for student learning in order to see the connection between writing and knowing that is so vital for understanding of writing across the curriculum. The mind-set that presents the highest hurdle for WAC planners is the same mind-set that governs the large lecture: "it is my job to present the material and it is their job to learn it," with *learn* an unconsidered term. Because this lack of thought about learning is so widespread among college faculty, it is indispensable that a WAC workshop for faculty focus early, through discussion and writing, on what we mean by *learning* and how our teaching can help bring it about.

The second stumbling block large classes present is the assumption by faculty that "my class is too large for me to assign writing." This assumption derives from the mistaken notion that *writing* can only mean conventional themes and term papers, meticulously scrutinized, marked up, and graded by the teacher. Knowing that this process is time-consuming and fraught with worry for the teacher who must agonize between granting a B– or a C+, faculty rightly fear the prospect of enduring this for 50 students, not to mention 200.

On the other hand, this fear, because it is so definite and strong, provides a great opportunity for the WAC workshop leader to present a fuller, liberating definition of *writing* and many refreshing alternatives to the conventional term paper torture. If the workshop leads the participants to make connections between writing and learning (as outlined by Britton; Martin et al.; Emig; and many others), then faculty will be open to such key ideas as writing not graded by the teacher, writing used for impromptu problem solving during classes, and writing shared by peers in small groups. Let teachers know that simply sharing with students a systematic way of taking notes and listening to lectures (e.g., Thaiss, *Write*, 58-60) can be a vital contribution to the WAC program.

If the workshop has also focused on writing as process (I recommend that leaders conduct some workshop exercises as processes of drafting, feedback, and revision so that participants get a feel for this; see Magnotto and Stout, this volume), then faculty will be open to seeing how they can ease their grading anxiety by making useful suggestions to early drafts rather than by devoting fruitless worried hours to marking and grading final drafts that the students have no chance to revise. If discussion of such techniques fails to ease faculty fears of the paper load, suggest such techniques as the "microtheme" developed at Montana State (Bean et al.), whereby students write brief essays, on note cards, in response to carefully limited questions.

In addition, emphasize writing that helps the teacher break down his or her own feelings of alienation in the impersonal lecture hall. In the alternative general education (PAGE) program at George Mason, we have had students write summaries and reviews of lectures in classes of more than 150, and keep these writings in portfolios that we regularly read through. These help us get to know the students, tune us in to what we need to clarify, and help us plan revisions of the course. As a variation, teachers can ask students to write questions about a lecture and use the student questions as the format for a subsequent class. Such exercises bridge the gap between teacher and students often imposed by the numbers and the lecture hall architecture.

While writing to learn can go on in important ways in the large class, no teacher in a large lecture can give to individuals the sustained attention to writing that real improvement either in style or in handling of ideas demands. So although the WAC planner for general education should never give in to the simple equation "large class = no writing," she needs to look for ways around or through the institutional structure to get students that attention. As a rule of thumb, always look for ways to break up large groups. If your institution varies the large lecture with discussion sections led by teaching assistants (TAs), consider putting strong emphasis on the training of TAs in WAC practices. Such institutions as UCLA have become models of this WAC emphasis (Strenski). In addition to seminars and workshops for TAs in WAC practice, UCLA's writing program publishes the *TA at UCLA Newsletter*, with articles written by TAs about such issues as assignment design and evaluation of papers.

Similarly, use the traditional structure of science lecture/laboratory courses to suggest to faculty the different types of writing and writing process appropriate to both venues. Focus on techniques like those described above, for example, microthemes, for the lecture; work with course planners and lab assistants to bring process theory into the writing of lab reports and the keeping of lab notebooks, as have faculty at such schools as Northern Iowa (Jensen) and Michigan Tech (Meese).

If a lecture course has no discussion sections, but has graders to assist the professor, suggest that these persons be trained in WAC theory and that their time be used to respond to the writing of subgroups of the students, with students given the opportunity to confer with the assistant and revise the work. If your institution supports no subdivision of the labor of the large class, do not stop pushing for it. Be inventive; adapt, for example, the writing fellows model developed at Brown (as described in Haring-Smith, this volume), whereby selected undergraduates are entrusted with responding to the drafts of students in classes across the disciplines. Or work with the writing center at your institution to have specially funded tutorial time allocated to specific large courses, as described in Harris (this volume). (Indeed, the writing center must be an integral part of any WAC program. At some schools, such as SUNY Albany, the WAC enterprise is directed through the center.)

General education planners should also explore the possibility of *linked* courses, one of which gives to writing as process the attention that the other, a large section, cannot give (see Graham, this volume). At Washington State, for example, large sections of world civilization are linked to small sections of composition, with students addressing in their journals and papers issues introduced in world civilization lectures and readings.

Finally, do not lose sight of the context of large and small classes within the general education frame. If the large class is more the exception than the rule in your general education setup, there may be no need to make the large class writing intensive (providing individual attention to drafts and requiring substantial numbers of pages), as long as other courses are providing this support for students. Focus the large class on the writing-to-learn techniques most doable and appropriate.

4. Courses Are Introductory or, in Some Programs, Interdisciplinary, so Students Lack Knowledge of Discourse and Methods in the Subject Area of the Course. The exciting convergence of literary theory, reading theory, and composing theory around the issue of discourse communities has key implications for how teachers view writing in the general education context. WAC planners need to take seriously the reading theorists' (e.g., Estes and Vaughan) exploration of "prior knowledge," the literary theorists' (e.g., Fish) assertion of specialized discourse, and the composing theorists' (e.g., Bartholomae) emphasis on students' slow learning of so-called academic discourse, because most faculty outside of composition classes have understandably given little thought to the often very esoteric nature of the good writing they'd like to expect from students: writing that shows an easy familiarity with the technical language and major issues of the discipline, a familiarity that can only be achieved over years of reading, writing, and conversation in the field. In WAC workshops with general education faculty, I stress this developmental process, lest faculty who are willing to assign writing in their classes drop out in frustration over the students' awkward prose and apparently sloppy use of key words. Although no writer can sidestep this movement through error to grace, teachers can apply process theory and use some writing-to-learn techniques that can further student development and ease their own frustration.

First, in their evaluation of student writings, faculty can learn to see the positive value in the student's attempts to use the language of the discipline and to achieve a professional tone. Faculty can learn to see through what might look like pompous or merely awkward writing to see the student's working with concepts and struggling to navigate unfamiliar terrain. Within the writing process, response to the student can focus on this intellectual effort rather than on clumsy style, which will improve with practice.

Second, workshop leaders should emphasize Emig's advice to writers to use their own language—language with which they are comfortable, rather than the technical prose of texts—to write about ideas they are trying to understand. In promoting the use of such writing-to-learn techniques as the learning log or brief, end-of-class summaries, teachers can use student samples that demonstrate the difference between thoughtful writing that uses words students know and writing that primarily tries to emulate the style of the textbook or the lecturer. It is vital for unsure students to know that they are allowed to use the familiar. For example, historian Betty Heycke of California State University-Chico assigns the following essay about late nineteenth-century American politics, this assignment designed to help students apply their reading without using textbook style.

> Write your brother about your daily life, your achievements, and your problems in America. You have, by the way, a pretty good idea of who is responsible for your financial problems and what should be done; and you have some strong opinions about the '96 Presidential election and the Populist Party. You think your brother needs to understand a little about American politics and economics to make his decision.

. . . Be specific. Use material from texts and lectures, *but do not quote the texts directly.* This must be in your own words (*Literacy and Learning* 3).

Indeed, one of the goals for general education in writing should be to develop students' ability to write for different discourse communities. One benefit of writing across the general education curriculum is to give students a taste of the conventional terms and formats of diverse fields. If writing occurs primarily in major courses, students often will not learn how to vary styles and assumptions as they vary their readers. One advantage of the LAN described earlier is that it brings into conversation students with varied interests and different levels of knowledge in a given subject. To contribute to the conversation, writers need to adjust style.

Sometimes this focus on diversifying discourse can be formalized in general education curriculum. At George Mason, an expressed purpose of the required junior-senior writing course is to give students practice in addressing specialized and nonspecialized readers. Students write research reports for readers (often the teachers of major courses) in their fields, then reuse the research data to write a different document for a different purpose to a nonspecialist. The heterogeneous (by majors) enrollment in a given section of the writing course allows for peer-response groups to be formed that give each writer practice in addressing lay readers.

Third, because students can only become familiar with diverse academic discourses through ongoing conversation with those "inside" the discourse, writers need feedback from teachers on drafts and some opportunities to revise. I suggest later that general education curricula should be set up to ensure that multidraft writing occurs in at least one course per semester.

Fourth, part of becoming familiar with academic discourse communities is to realize that there are many such communities and many modes of writing that we can call academic. A good question to ask in a faculty workshop is "What do professionals in your field write?" A useful second question is "Do students in our general education courses get some exposure to these types of writing and some practice doing them?" Invite faculty to bring to the workshop samples of typical documents and have them brainstorm ways to give general education students some practice in doing what professionals do. A WAC program that includes collecting and analyzing data in a science lab, composing program notes for a musical performance, keeping a field log in sociology, and comparing first-person accounts of an historical event in a history class more practically teaches writers versatility than do the artificial exercises in modes of discourse that still characterize many composition classes. These "professional practice" assignments need not be elaborate to be significant; for example, sociologist Keith Crew of Northern Iowa sees the essay exams he gives his introductory students (he formerly gave multiple-choice tests) as vital training in the "sociological imagination" (3).

5. In Four-Year Colleges and Universities, Faculty Who Teach General Education Tend to Have Less Experience, Less Job Security, and Less Chance to Communicate With Other Faculty Than Those Who Teach Major Courses. Addressing WAC in general education forces many institutions to address their inequities in hiring and compensation. The four-year college or university that gives stipends or release time for WAC participation only to regular faculty systematically ignores WAC in general education, if that school uses adjuncts or TAs as the main teaching cadres at the freshman-sophomore level. I've heard it argued that giving workshop stipends to nonregular faculty is not cost effective, because these faculty are not likely to stay at the institution. But is it more cost-effective, in terms of the needs of general education, to give extra money to a full-timer who neither teaches general education courses nor is likely to have much contact with those who do?

If a school wants to upgrade WAC in its general education courses, WAC planners need to look closely at present and future staffing. Despite the strong wishes of department chairs, is it likely that those 25 part-time FTE will be turned into 25 tenure-track slots? Or is it more likely that those 15 adjuncts who have been with the school for the past eight years will be there for the next eight, despite the low prestige, including low pay? Is it equally likely that the full-time equivalent (FTE) for TAs, which grew to 15 in 1985 and 20 in 1988, might become 25 by 1993? If your institutional trend has been that fewer and fewer regular faculty are teaching general education, and if your administration has expressed some commitment to WAC in general education, push your funders to get stipends and other compensation for the people who'll be doing the teaching and for those regular faculty who have already demonstrated commitment to freshmen and sophomores. Particularly in schools that stress full-timers' research and their directing of graduate students, it is cost-effective to put WAC dollars for general education into workshops for adjuncts and TAs. Such money is necessary compensation for adjuncts who otherwise have no contractual obligation to do more than teach their classes, and it can inspire commitment to the institution, despite the poor conditions under which adjuncts normally work.

As for TAs, WAC money can be used for release time for leaders of training programs, as it is at Harvard, Cornell (Bogel and Gottschalk), UCLA, Syracuse, Ohio State, and a number of other research universities. As long as a significant number of introductory classes, discussion sections, labs, and other occasions for writing in general education are handled by TAs, faculty development money must be spent there, even though the TAs will be taking their skills elsewhere in one or two years. Such spending not only benefits the undergraduate program but makes the graduate program more attractive to students looking to enhance their teaching credentials.

6. The Goals of General Education Courses Tend to Be Broad and Idealistic—e.g., "Cultural Literacy," "The Ability to Write in College," "Appreciation of Scientific Method"—Whereas the Goals of Major Courses Tend to Be Narrow and Preprofessional.

The breadth of general education goals at most campuses reflects the uncertainty of faculties about just what our students need to know and do as educated citizens. Campus debates, such as those surrounding the Stanford core, feature urgent complaints about the students' ignorance of history, global interrelations, scientific method, math at all levels, ethics and morals, the arts, cultural diversity, and much else. These debates often lead to new courses, with most faculty attention paid to which authors will be required reading and which topics will show up on sample syllabi.

But because such curricula emerge out of debate of widely differing positions, and because the courses, whatever their shape on paper, will be taught by diverse people with diverse agendas, every general education program has lots of room for experimentation. This makes general education fun for the WAC planner, and indicates a workshop design that promotes imaginative thinking and a multitude of individual plans. In a general education WAC workshop, one should give participants plenty of time to invent assignments and to discuss them. Faculty can work both individually and in small groups to brainstorm exciting options.

As facilitator, your primary job is to record and display what the participants create. Because you have done the thinking about writing process that most of them have not, your equally important task is to push them to consider the process implications of their ideas. For example, let's say that participants teaching a course on Western intellectual history since the Renaissance show enthusiasm for a project that asks students to role-play a Marxist critic and a Freudian critic giving reviews of Dickens's *Hard Times*. Use that enthusiasm to start a discussion of their expectations of the students: How will they handle students' intimidation by the task? How will they respond to drafts? How can they involve the students themselves in the creation of criteria and in responding to their peers? Is it necessary for this project to be a multidraft paper, or could the role-play work as a series of log entries? This workshop design lets the participants generate the content and takes advantage of the creative, experimental nature of general education. It also lets the workshop leader avoid playing the expert from on high who is telling them the assignments, criteria, and processes to build into the courses. This design takes full advantage, nevertheless, of the leader's expertise in WAC theory and practice.

If one of the goals of general education at your school is "competence in reading and writing," or something of that nature, the vagueness again allows freedom, although I hasten to add that the presence of such a goal, albeit vague, at most schools shows college teachers' recognition of the importance of literacy. Indeed, almost all interest in WAC is occasioned by this concern. Nevertheless, the vagueness of the goal means that there will be on any campus much uncertainty about the details of competence and how it might be measured. An important job for any WAC planner is to address this unformed, though often intense, concern through information and through careful discussion of the issues underlying the growth and assessment of competence (see Greenberg et al. for a range of ideas on writing assessment by institutions).

If faculty at your school have shown concern about competence, use this concern as the nexus for your workshops. In a recent workshop for core curriculum faculty at George Mason, teachers representing several departments engaged in reading of sample student papers to determine and prioritize their criteria for competence. This exercise led to discussion of the larger issue of course objectives and how writing can help students meet those objectives. Following the "primary traits" workshop and several days of course-team meetings, faculty produced not only refined sets of course objectives but also inventive ideas for writing assignments clearly linked to the objectives.

In all WAC workshops, I continue to find it useful to show how the British research of the sixties and seventies (e.g., Britton; Martin et al.) that grew into the WAC movement originated in national concern about literacy. Discussion of this research both assures the participants that many professionals have shared their concerns and introduces such key WAC concepts as *writing process* and *writing to learn* as well as opening up connections between writing and the other language modes. Keep in mind that it is possible to begin a WAC workshop at any stage of the writing process, as long as that stage addresses a concern of the participants. If a faculty group is deeply concerned about evaluation of writing, you can begin with an evaluation of sample papers and let the diversity of responses and criteria that emerge lead the group to investigate how one builds assignments, teaches criteria, helps students give feedback to one another, writes comments on drafts, and so on. The workshop leader acts mainly as a resource, suggesting techniques from the literature in response to questions.

7. Most General Education Requirements Come in Three- or Six-Hour Chunks; There Is Neither Continuity From One Chunk to Another nor Any Explicit Connection Between Them. Not only do students enter general education courses without intrinsic motivation (Tendency 1) and with little or no savvy about the discourse of the subject area (Tendency 4) but the courses students take for general education credit usually appear to students to be so many unrelated fragments. This fragmentation doesn't usually trouble students, because they're used to it from high school, where they were also expected to complete courses that other people had chosen for them and that were rarely presented as if they had anything to do with one another. But this state does trouble faculty who have a vision of a coherent general education, one that students can integrate into their lives during and beyond school. These teachers know that we can't be motivated to learn without a sense of how new information fits with what we already care about. New information that we can't fit into a context we either won't perceive at all or we'll forget as soon as the immediate context, the course, is over. As general education students, we get to be pretty good at keeping alive the names, dates, symbols, and formulas just long enough to pass the final.

One reason WAC has become popular at campuses is that faculty recognize that writing is too useful to be thought of as a fragment. They affirm that written words are the glue that can hold the fragments together. Most faculty readily buy the argument that students will not learn to write well if they write only in the required composition course(s). They also readily agree that if the students do not learn to write well, our verbal-dependent civilization will crumble.

What the WAC workshop can do is help faculty see how writing can help bring about that ideal of the coherent general education. In the PAGE program at George Mason, years of experience have taught us that merely making interdisciplinary courses does not mean students will perceive the interconnectedness of their courses. If one assumes that general education courses are fragments, then it is just as easy to see as unrelated fragments two seminars called Technology in Society and Environmental Problems as it is Biology 101 and Sociology 101. If we want to substitute the paradigm of connectedness for the paradigm of fragmentation, we have to explicitly stress connecting in how we teach. How can writing help?

Informally, in a learning log or in-class exercise, I can ask students to speculate possible connections between ideas in my course and ideas in one or more other courses they are taking. I like to be honest with the class about why I'm asking this: Making these connections will help them see all the courses as more meaningful and give more purpose to our collective enterprise. They do not want to waste their time or their money, and thinking connectedly will ensure that that doesn't happen. *Connections* writing can be a standard part of a course log or an occasional assignment. Some students will catch on more quickly than others, so it is useful to share with a class one or two particularly fine examples from students or devote a bit of class time to small- or large-group discussion of ideas students have come up with.

Such informal "writing to connect" can lead to more formal projects. Let's say that a student in my section of the American literature survey has noted that the readings on slavery in his American history course influenced his reading of *Huckleberry Finn*. Either the history professor or I can suggest a fuller exploration of this connection in a multidraft paper. Through such assignments, not only do we make writing cross-curricular but literature, history, and the other subjects students choose to connect become cross-curricular, too.

THINKING PROGRAMMATICALLY

A WAC workshop devoted to general education can be as course centered or as program centered as participants wish. Faculty will always be interested in the methods they use in their own classes, so a large part of any workshop will focus on writing in that context. But we can't really deal with WAC in general education unless we have participants spend some time seeing their own classes in the context of all the requirements. As I suggested above in my discussion of class size, programmatic thinking can save us the anxiety of trying to turn the large lecture into a writing-intensive course, because a look at the entire distribution of courses will show us where that structure is more appropriate. Similarly, programmatic thinking will help any faculty workshop group achieve a balanced, varied writing experience for students. For example, because journals and logs have proven fairly easy to implement in many contexts (see Fulwiler), WAC programs can unwittingly inflict "journal overkill" on students, with students keeping three or more logs in a semester. We encountered this problem at George Mason not long after the establishment of PAGE in 1982. Consequently, it became a recurring theme of our annual faculty workshops to plan a diverse, complementary writing program across the curriculum. In one semester, for example, students would keep a journal in one course, would do a multistage library/interview research paper in another, would prepare collaborative fieldwork projects in a third, and in a fourth would keep a log that asked them to integrate ideas from the other courses. Programmatic thinking might also coax participants to consider, for example, a combined journal for two or more courses, or a portfolio of occasional ungraded writings instead of the more conventional log.

The size of your general education program and the number of faculty involved in teaching it, plus the amount of administrative release the program allows, will determine how tightly planned and supervised the writing experiences can be. George Mason's PAGE program (see Appendix to this chapter), with several hundred students and faculty teams of six or eight per each of 12 courses, specifies writing assignments for each section of every course. By contrast, the core curriculum at Brooklyn College (see Appendix to this chapter), which serves thousands of students per year, relies on each faculty member to determine the "nature of the assignments" and specifies only that some assignments in each course be short and that students receive feedback to help them improve their abilities "to think clearly and write well." The Brooklyn core also provides some continuity between freshman English and the other core courses by faculty agreement to use the same set of correction and improvement symbols (*Introduction* 7).

As a WAC planner, you can monitor the diversity of writing in your general education program and work with your faculty individually and in workshops to achieve balance. In workshops, record and display the ideas for implementing WAC that the participants create. Suggest that the group examine the list for balance and diversity:

Do students have regular opportunities in most general education courses to do ungraded writing-to-learn exercises of some kind?

Are writing-to-learn assignments varied between regular log keeping outside of class (in one or two courses a semester) and primarily in-class assignments in other courses?

Do students take at the very least one course per semester in which they write one or more multidraft papers that receive response in process from the teacher or peers?

Are assignments varied to give students practice with some of the diverse types of writing that professionals do in the fields that students encounter in general education, for example, archival research in history, collection and analysis of data in labs, field-work log keeping in the social sciences?

Do students get opportunities to write for audiences besides the teacher— peers, professionals, the public?

If variety is lacking, ask the faculty to brainstorm for some alternatives.

When you work with faculty individually, try to balance your sense of the students' needs for a varied writing experience and your sense of the writing appropriate to the given course. If I'm encountering the third person in a row who has the students keep a learning log, I like to listen to how the person describes the log and the rationale for it before I suggest an alternative. If the requirement sounds interesting and well thought out, I'll happily applaud it and feel lucky for the students who have this teacher. If the requirement sounds merely conventional, I'll not hesitate to suggest alternatives that seem to me better suited to the course. This goes for other requirements besides journals, too, especially research papers and essay exams, which faculty often require out of a general sense of obligation to support writing, rather than out of imaginative thinking about students' needs either in writing experience or in learning of the course subject.

Maybe the greatest benefit of programmatic thinking about writing in general education is that you can help faculty design a program of writing for all students that doesn't overburden either student or faculty, that gives the students a well-conceived general education in writing, and that enables faculty to feel that they are contributing to students' overall growth without feeling the anxiety of "not doing enough." The teacher who sees that others are attending to close editing of students' prose will not feel constrained to do the same, and thus will spend more time happily writing comments that nurture the seeds of original thinking. If the thoughtful use of writing in our introductory courses can help our students think critically and creatively, make connections among their seemingly disparate courses, and feel connected to the school, then all our general education planning will have been worth the effort.

APPENDIX

The following are core course requirements in the Plan for Alternative General Education (PAGE) at George Mason University and in the core curriculum at Brooklyn College.

George Mason University PAGE Curriculum

Semester 1
    Computers in Contemporary Society (4 credits)
    Reading the Arts (3 credits)
    Conceptions of the Self (3 credits)
    Symbols, Codes, and Information I (1 credit)
    Values, Themes, and Cultural Problems I (1 credit)
Semester 2
    Analysis and Solution of Quantitative Problems I (3 credits)
    Reading Cultural Signs (3 credits)
    Contemporary Society in Multiple Perspectives (3 credits)
    Symbols, Codes, and Information II (1 credit)
    Values, Themes, and Cultural Problems II (1 credit)
Semester 3
    Analysis and Solution of Quantitative Problems II (3 credits)
    Scientific Thought and Processes I (4 credits)
    Cross-Cultural Perspectives (3 credits)
    Symbols, Codes, and Information III (1 credit)
    Values, Themes, and Cultural Problems III (1 credit)
Semester 4
    Scientific Thought and Processes II (4 credits)
    The Decision-Making Process and the Choice of Technologies (3
        credits)
    The Contemporary United States (3 credits)

Brooklyn College Core Curriculum (from *Introduction*)

First Tier
    Core Studies 1: Classical Origins of Western Culture
    Core Studies 2: Introduction to Art
    Core Studies 2: Introduction to Music
    Core Studies 3: People, Power, and Politics
    Core Studies 4: The Shaping of the Modern World
    Core Studies 5: Introduction to Mathematical Reasoning and Com-
        puter Programming

Second Tier

Core Studies 6: Landmarks of Literature

Core Studies 7: Science in Modern Life I (Chemistry, Physics)

Core Studies 8: Science in Modern Life II (Biology, Geology)

Core Studies 9: Studies in African, Asian, and Latin American Cultures

Core Studies 10: Knowledge, Existence, and Values

Foreign Language Study through Level 3 or equivalent proficiency.

WORKS CITED

Bartholomae, David. "Wandering: Misreadings, Miswritings, and Misunderstandings." *Only Connect: Uniting Reading and Writing.* Ed. Thomas Newkirk. Portsmouth, NH: Boynton, 1986. 89-118.

Bean, John C., et al. "Microtheme Strategies for Developing Cognitive Skills." *Teaching Writing in All Disciplines.* Ed. C. W. Griffin. San Francisco: Jossey-Bass, 1982. 27-38.

Bogel, Frederic V., and Katherine Gottschalk, eds. *Teaching Prose: A Guide for Writing Instructors.* New York: Norton, 1988.

Britton, James. *Language and Learning.* Harmondsworth, UK: Penguin, 1970. Available from Boynton.

Crew, Keith. "Writing Processes and the Sociological Imagination." *Cross-Over: A WAC Newsletter.* Fall 1989: 3-6.

Emig, Janet. "Writing as a Mode of Learning." *College Composition and Communication* 28 (1977): 122-128. Rpt. in *The Writing Teacher's Sourcebook.* Ed. Gary Tate and Edward Corbett: 85-91. New York: Oxford, 1981.

Estes, Thomas, and Joseph Vaughn. *Reading and Reasoning Beyond the Primary Grades.* Boston: Allyn, 1986.

Fish, Stanley. *Is There a Text in This Class? The Authority of Interpretive Communities.* Cambridge, MA: Harvard, 1980.

Fulwiler, Toby, ed. *The Journal Book.* Portsmouth, NH: Boynton, 1987.

Greenberg, Karen L., et al. *Writing Assessment: Issues and Strategies.* New York: Longman, 1986.

"History by the Letter," *Literacy and Learning: Newsletter of the Writing Across the Disciplines Program.* California State University, Chino, Feb. 1990. 3.

Introduction to the Core Curriculum. Brooklyn College, 1985.

Jensen, Verner. "Writing in College Physics." *The Journal Book.* Ed. Toby Fulwiler. Portsmouth, NH: Boynton, 1987. 330-36.

Katz, Joseph, et al. *A New Vitality in General Education.* Washington, DC: Association of American Colleges, 1988.

Literacy and Learning. Feb. 1990. Newsletter of the Writing Across the Disciplines Program, California State University/Chico.

Martin, Nancy, et al. *Writing and Learning Across the Curriculum, 11-16*. London: Ward Lock, 1976. Available from Boynton.

Meese, George. "Focused Learning in Chemistry Research: Suzanne's Journal." *The Journal Book*. Ed. Toby Fulwiler. Portsmouth, NH: Boynton, 1987. 337-47.

Nielsen, Anne. "Reading, Writing, and Reactions in Biology 101." Virginia Community College System Conference. Roanoke, Apr. 1988.

Singer, Marti. "Responding to Intimacies and Crises in Students' Journals." *The English Journal* 79 (Sept. 1990): 72-75.

Strenski, Ellen. "Writing Across the Curriculum at Research Universities." *Strengthening Programs for Writing Across the Curriculum*. Ed. Susan McLeod. San Francisco: Jossey-Bass, 1988. 31-41.

Thaiss, Christopher, et al. "WAC at George Mason University." *Programs That Work*. Ed. Toby Fulwiler and Art Young. Portsmouth, NH: Boynton, 1990. 221-42.

———. *Write to the Limit*. Fort Worth: Holt, 1991.

EIGHT

Writing Components, Writing Adjuncts, Writing Links

JOAN GRAHAM

Writing to learn is a readily reversible phrase: It names a way of learning to write. When students engage in learning new concepts and information, articulating questions, insights, problems, and possibilities, their activities amount to the generation of content for writing. And writing well inevitably depends in some degree on content, on what a writer has to say.

Often writing teachers want to focus on content concerns, to strengthen students' ability to generate and manage new thoughts—but their teaching contexts have made such a focus difficult to achieve. In a traditional, freestanding writing class, considerable time must be spent discussing a subject for writing and defining as well as possible the audience and purpose that writing should serve. Yet despite much effort students may perceive writing course assignments as mere exercises, rather than as writing occasions of value in themselves. In so far as writing subjects seem arbitrary, readings or activities to develop subjects seem thin, or writing purposes seem artificial or vague, students are likely to make only shallow investment in the content of what they write.

It is partly the need for better opportunities to teach writing as engagement in inquiry that has led to new curriculum arrangements and new course designs. Innovations are addressing the traditional organization of academe, which has separated writing instruction from the contexts and occasions where students need to write. Writing teachers have always had instructional time and expertise to offer, but the inquiry contexts they could create have often been weak. Subject discipline teachers have always created strong inquiry contexts but they have had little or no time for writing instruction and may have lacked expertise. New, deliberate integration of teaching scenes is an opportunity to strengthen the impact of instruction on both sides. Although the most common WAC activities stress the use of writing to serve learning in a subject discipline, the emphasis is also being reversed: Subject discipline courses are helping students learn to write via writing components, writing adjuncts, and writing links.

These departures from the freestanding writing course all put writing instruction in the context of students' study in particular lecture courses. The disciplines represented by lecture courses are important frames, but the focus is on immediate experience—on the questions and purposes that define individual courses as they unfold. Typically, writing instructors sit in on their students' lecture classes and treat them as discourse communities, developing writing activities that capitalize on the readings, conceptual frameworks and problems that students share.

All the designs for integrating work on writing with subject discipline study dramatize the importance of writers' contexts and so are fundamentally related. Such designs might be said to vary according to the amount of instructional time each makes available, and the "place" where work goes on. First would come writing centers, where students get optional, individual consultation with tutors on work in progress for any course (see Harris, this volume; Hilgers and Marsella); then would come writing fellows programs, in which designated tutors provide required consultation for all students in a particular lecture course as they prepare essay drafts (see Haring-Smith, this volume). Next there is a shift from consultation to instruction as additional academic credit recognizes additional class time devoted to writing concerns. Distinguishing consultation from instruction is a little misleading, because consultation as a basic feature continues, students meeting with writing teachers to discuss ideas and drafts when a lecture course has a distinct writing component or when it is accompanied by an adjunct or a link. But class meetings are added in these cases. Class meetings give students the opportunity to see and learn from each other's written work, and they allow for a wider range of writing issues and activities—all, of course, making use of shared materials and experiences from a lecture class.

The terms *component, adjunct,* and *link* are not used across institutions in fully consistent ways, but I am adopting these terms because in many cases they do represent a considered choice, and they help me make some important distinctions here. Writing components are least autonomous, as the label suggests. Components are typically part of a core program or course: Core courses with a distinct writing component carry more credit than regular lecture courses, but the writing component is not a separate course. Writing adjuncts and writing links are separate courses, attached to lecture courses but not part of them. Both adjuncts and links are in some cases optional, in other cases required. But adjuncts and links are different from each other in credit weight— different in a way that has substantive consequences as well as political effects. An adjunct typically meets half as much time and carries half as much credit as the lecture course it accompanies, whereas *link* indicates a writing course that matches a lecture course, meeting an equal amount of time and carrying equal credit weight.

Integrated writing instruction of some type is potentially valuable in a wide variety of contexts—for basic writers or for honors students, with general education courses or with majors' courses, involving discipline faculty in greater or in lesser degree. But successful integration requires administrators' patience, writing teachers' interest, and a design that will serve well-considered aims.

Among the questions to be answered:

1. Should components or adjuncts or links be developed? At what level? Will they be optional or required? How will they relate to existing institutional requirements?

2. If components are chosen, will existing lecture courses be modified or will new courses be designed? Similarly if adjuncts or links are chosen, will they be companions to existing lecture courses? Or will lecture courses be modified or new courses be designed?

3. Who will the writing instructors and the discipline lecturers be? How many will be needed to begin, and how will they be selected? What

incentives will be offered? How much preliminary training will be needed? Ongoing support?

4. How much interaction will be required between writing instructors and discipline lecturers as courses are taught? Who will manage course coordination? Who will be responsible to whom for what?

5. How will students learn about integrated writing instruction—what it is, where to find it, how to register?

6. How will components or adjuncts or links be evaluated?

Because initiating integrated writing instruction may require many decisions, it is common for programs to start small. It is also common for integration designs to change, new patterns displacing or adding to the originals. Initial decisions cannot be made piecemeal for they are related to each other—and also to the problems and priorities of institutions. Such larger forces also underlie program expansions and changes. Of course a simple list of questions cannot suggest these things, so I am going to describe some particular institutions' plans and experiences with program development.

COMPONENTS: UC SAN DIEGO

Integrated writing instruction began at UC San Diego's Third College in the fall of 1991. The new program, titled "Dimensions of Culture," makes writing a key component in a three-quarter sequence of core courses, the sequence to be required for all 600 freshmen. This concept for curriculum reform has been awaiting attention for some time, and now a strongly interested provost is helping to implement it (Cooper).

Previously, Third College offered a first-year composition course and also writing adjuncts attached to 12 sophomore-level general education courses. Faculty believed, however, that choosing among 12 courses—the menu approach to general education—did not ensure a common intellectual experience for incoming students. They believed that a newly designed, unified core course sequence would allow students to gain that common intellectual experience, and as an additional benefit, writing-to-learn strategies could be developed more systematically for a core course sequence than for 12 separate courses for which frequent changes in faculty and teaching assistants were involved. Now that writing instruction has been placed in the context of students' common core course sequence, Third College no longer offers a separate composition course.

Each quarter, the core course involves three discipline lecturers and enough teaching assistants (TAs) to lead small discussion and writing sections. The intellectual approach and continuity of the three-quarter core course was planned by a faculty committee chaired by Michael Schudson, a professor in the communication department. Faculty lecturers in each quarter develop a common syllabus and select readings and films. In 1991-92, faculty came from five departments: communication, political science, history, anthropology, ethnic studies, and literature.

The role of writing in the core courses is at first limited. During fall quarter, students hear three lectures and participate in one discussion section each week. Although they write journal responses to course readings, no class time or course credit is allowed for work with writing because of a special University of California rule: Mandatory first-quarter freshman courses cannot involve writing "instruction" because some entering students will not be eligible, i.e., they will not yet have passed the basic requirement known as "Subject A." Winter and spring quarters bring full implementation of the core course writing component. Students participate in two section meetings each week, and the core courses carry six credits per quarter instead of the usual four.

Charles Cooper and Susan Peck McDonald coordinate the core program, hire and supervise TAs, lead a weekly TA seminar, and work closely with faculty lecturers to develop paper topics for core courses in winter and spring. The TAs who lead winter and spring sections are given released time in the fall, so they can read course materials for the coming quarters, attend the seminar in which materials are discussed, and help develop section activities. Lecturing faculty provide consultation in the seminar, which is designed to give TAs from seven departments (as of 1991-92) their own common intellectual experience. The TAs also gain some insight into writing pedagogy, and ways that writing can further learning. In the sections TAs lead, students address frequent, brief writing-to-learn assignments and write essay exams; students also write papers, conferring with their TAs as they produce drafts and revisions.

As for what students write about, the core lecturers focus on large social issues, like justice and diversity. Each of the three faculty members working with the core course in a given quarter lectures to a class of about 200 students, and all three classes have the same syllabus and readings. But it remains to be seen exactly how alike the classes are, given that one lecturer might be a historian and another an anthropologist. The core sequence is intended to be interdisciplinary, but as classes struggle with ways of defining problems and ways of evaluating evidence, disciplinary perspectives will almost certainly have some effects—and those effects may become evident in the writing students produce. It is common that, when writing instruction is integrated, both writing specialists and subject discipline lecturers learn from the experience, and such learning may be especially important in this case.

In programs that offer writing instruction in companion courses (i.e., adjuncts or links), the signs of disciplinary perspectives in lecture courses are usually exploited as discovery tools rather than effaced. But it takes time for writing students to recognize, employ, and reflect on the purposes and methods of a discipline course, and the time available in an adjunct is quite limited. Adjuncts have proved valuable in a number of ways, but partly because these classes have so little meeting time, they have tended to produce less lasting satisfaction than links. Changes have been under way for some time in the UCLA adjunct program, for example, and changes are expected soon in the UC Santa Barbara program as well.

ADJUNCTS: UCLA AND UC SANTA BARBARA

At UCLA, writing program faculty have offered a wide variety of adjuncts, two-credit English courses attached to lecture courses in many fields (see Cullen). But the number of adjuncts offered was down to about eight per quarter by 1990-91, less than one-third the number offered when the program was at its height. This reduction results from both negative and positive aspects of accrued experience. On the negative side, the institution has recently had to make many cuts in course offerings not required for graduation; in the writing program, cuts fell on the adjuncts partly because they are administratively more demanding than other courses. That is, they are harder to schedule, monitor, and evaluate than freestanding courses. Also, staffing adjuncts well is sometimes difficult, for teachers of adjuncts (like teachers of links) must be willing to work with discourses outside their own field. So the special administrative requirements of adjuncts, as well as long-felt frustration with the amount of teaching time they provide, worked against maintenance of many offerings (Strenski).

There was also a quite different, positive reason for cutting many adjuncts: in a certain sense, their work was done. At UCLA, adjuncts were used deliberately as a way to raise discipline faculty consciousness about writing issues and to cultivate better use of writing in teaching across the curriculum. Writing teachers who offered adjuncts came to know well the materials and aims of the discipline lecture courses essential to their own work, and so they were exceptionally well prepared to serve as writing consultants to their lecturing colleagues. The use of writing in many lecture courses has been influenced by the faculty interaction that came with past adjuncts—and the effects continue, although adjuncts themselves may have disappeared.

Some effects of adjuncts are, in fact, a physical presence. In-house guides to writing in several disciplines were produced by collaborating teachers, and they are widely used. Codifying faculty methods of using writing in teaching, the guides derived directly from the adjunct experience—neither discipline faculty nor English faculty could have written them alone. The guides are also an influence now in the wider academic community: The guide to writing in sociology, for example, is in its second edition, published by St. Martin's Press.

As I've suggested, some adjuncts do continue to be offered at UCLA, but as of winter 1992, they carry four credits—in effect, they have become links. Among the adjuncts (links) that continue are those accompanying certain lecture courses in sociology, for which majors in the field must satisfy a requirement by taking one. The move to increase credits was made because UCLA's first experiment with four-credit adjuncts (links)—part of a special program for transfer students—was such a success.

The Transfer Intensive Program (TIP) is for students who have fulfilled the UCLA composition requirement, but whose transition to UCLA study will be aided by some concentrated work with analytical reading and writing. The program makes available four-credit, upper-division writing classes in conjunction with a specified lecture course on the general education list. The program also provides designated counselors who are familiar with the needs of transfer students, and the counselors stay in touch with TIP writing instructors.

Finally, UCLA's adjunct experience is contributing in various ways to new offerings in writing pedagogy and in preprofessional programs. For example, the new Community Educator Project (CEP) is intended "to interest nontraditional students in careers in education." Designed by representatives of three units—the Academic Advancement Program, Writing Programs, and the Field Studies Office—CEP consists of a year-long sequence of specially designed composition courses that are "adjuncted with" fieldwork. CEP students study the "social and personal impact of education," engaging in various activities that foster reading, writing and critical thinking skill. Furthermore, they apply what they learn and make their own observations by working as tutors for elementary and secondary students in several area schools. Connecting writing instruction with this fieldwork is a powerful way to help students articulate, analyze, and evaluate what they see.

Experiences with writing adjuncts at UC Santa Barbara in some ways overlap with those at UCLA, but in other ways they are distinct. The Santa Barbara program is only about half as old, having begun in 1985, but it expanded very rapidly to offer adjuncts with lectures in 22 departments in just two years. At present, the program offers 15 to 18 adjunct classes per quarter for a year total of about 50 (Zimmerman).

Writing instructors have usually held only part of their appointment in the adjunct program, but Santa Barbara has had more opportunity than UCLA to select teachers specifically for adjunct work. On the other hand, interaction between adjunct teachers and discipline lecturers has been much less a feature of the Santa Barbara program. Although there have, of course, been cases where writing teachers played a consultant's role, the Santa Barbara situation virtually required that this be a matter of individual teachers' tastes and opportunities, not a programmatic expectation. While at UCLA it was assumed that adjuncts should influence lecture courses, at Santa Barbara assurances were needed that lecture courses would *not* have to change.

Of course, many probably made good use of writing already. To find lectures with which to place adjuncts, director Muriel Zimmerman began by simply calling undergraduate program secretaries in various departments and asking which department faculty members were known to assign a lot of writing in their courses. Discipline lecturers were usually happy to have adjuncts arranged, for they seemed a practical, intellectually rigorous kind of instruction, and the association of two classes could be expected to enhance students' motivation.

After five years of mainly positive experience, however, changes are coming as all Santa Barbara writing programs are reorganized. It is likely that the change for adjuncts will be a quite straightforward strengthening: Their credit weight will be doubled as these courses are, in effect, made into links. It was apparent to some when the program began that two-credit adjuncts could not make full use of the opportunities that paired courses present, for the adjuncts would meet for only an hour and 15 minutes a week. But that arrangement was what was politically feasible at the time, and it was a way to make a start. Now, besides broadly inclusive changes in the organization of writing programs, new upper- and lower-division writing requirements are being put in place. More resources are being made available, too: Those resources will allow new four-credit adjuncts (effectively links) to be developed as an appropriate way to fulfill requirements. In addition to those for upper-division students, approximately 10 classes for freshmen will be piloted in fall 1992.

LINKS: UC DAVIS, UNC AT CHAPEL HILL, AND UNIVERSITY OF WASHINGTON

Among schools that already have writing link programs in place are the University of California at Davis, the University of North Carolina at Chapel Hill, and the University of Washington. The program at UC Davis is an activity of the Campus Writing Center, and it offers about 15 classes per quarter. Links accompany lectures in a variety of disciplines but all at the upper-division level, and students who take them must already have satisfied a lower-division writing requirement. The links do considerable work with academic styles and with documentation issues in particular disciplines; they also regularly make real-world assignments.

The UC Davis program would like to add lower-division links with general education lectures, so that students would begin to experience the ways discourse communities vary as part of their fundamental instruction in writing. At present, general education courses are supposed to be writing intensive, but discussion sections provide only small opportunity for writing instruction, and TAs who lead sections need more training. The Campus Writing Center is playing an increasing role in departments' TA training programs, and training with respect to writing is made as discipline and course specific as possible. But more needs to be done. Development of lower-division writing links is part of the long-term plan, because that could contribute not only to the curriculum but to TA training as well. New writing-focused workshops to help prepare "the new professoriate" have already begun, and one-unit adjuncts are being considered as companions to some graduate courses (Palo).

The writing link program at the UNC Chapel Hill is relatively new, and it has set out deliberately to address TA training in the context of course development. The origins of the program are in the work of an ad hoc committee of the faculty council, which was asked to look into WAC in the mid-eighties. That committee identified two contexts of concern: medium-size classes, where lecturers interacted directly with students, and large classes where students' contact was mostly with TAs. Then, in 1987, UNC Chapel Hill received from the Ford Foundation a Dean's Grant in Literacy and the Liberal Arts. Grant funds were used to begin addressing needs in the two contexts already identified. Workshops were made available for faculty teaching medium-size courses, and a new program was created to pair large lectures with writing links (Lindemann).

The large lectures are an integral program element, for they are offered by discipline faculty willing to serve as team leaders— teams being composed of TAs in the discipline who will lead discussion sections and also TAs from English who will teach writing links. The design is like the one at UC San Diego in two ways: Lectures are created as program elements rather than simply chosen from existing curriculum, and all students who take program lectures also take writing concurrently. The designs are different in two ways as well: The UNC Chapel Hill lecture courses are discipline defined rather than interdisciplinary, and Chapel Hill provides links with lectures (equal meeting time, equal credit weight and separate grades) rather than components of lectures (less proportional time and no separate status as a graded unit). It should also be noted that UC San Diego will be offering a course sequence, whereas the UNC Chapel Hill courses last one semester.

So far, Chapel Hill lecturers in sociology, history, psychology and philosophy, geography, and astronomy have developed introductory courses for this program, although competing demands on faculty time have allowed no more than five of the courses to be offered in a given semester. Each lecture course is accompanied by 4 or 5 writing links, so the total number of links offered at a time is about 20. The English TAs who teach the links usually have some background, perhaps even an undergraduate major, in the lecture discipline. These TAs are selected by writing program administrators on the basis of applications and interviews. Writing assignments made in the links might include case studies, literature reviews, data problems, or analyses of primary documents as well as essays on ideas or events—students work in whatever genres are appropriate for a given discipline.

Preparation for fall lecture courses and writing links begins with week-long workshops held each year in May. The workshops are convened by the discipline faculty members serving as team leaders—people interested in offering freshman courses and sensitive to writing/learning issues. Both TAs who will lead discussion sections and TAs who will teach writing links take part in the workshops; faculty and TAs receive stipends for this period of concentrated planning work. The teams also meet periodically during the semester in which they teach, but what is crucial is the shared experience of the initial workshops.

As a curriculum feature, Chapel Hill's writing links are highly successful, and as a training occasion for future faculty both in English and in the disciplines they are obviously of great value. There would seem to be just two important limitations to the design: First, it requires discipline faculty willing and able to offer appropriate freshman courses and serve as team leaders. Given the many competing demands that faculty face, the number of lecture and writing link teams may never be large. Second, the

May workshops are expensive. But the demand for this kind of integrated instruction is obvious. According to former writing program director Erika Lindemann, freshmen who entered in the fall of 1988 learned about the new courses from a notice in the registration materials they were sent. Included in those materials was a card to be returned immediately if a student wanted to be enrolled in a lecture and writing link set. Requests would be granted in the order received until enrollment limits were met, and the program designers simply had no idea what the response would be. As it turned out, of 3,200 cards sent, 3,000 were returned. Almost the entire incoming class wanted writing instruction in the context of lecture course study. Some students returned their cards by Federal Express.

Although the number of links currently offered hardly meets the demand, the new courses are influencing old offerings, helping to bring changes in the freshman English program as a whole. Jim Williams, the current program director, has redefined the focus of the two semester-long general composition courses. The concept of writing communities now underlies both, the fall course immersing students in writers' contexts outside of academe, the spring course turning to the major divisions inside academe— writing in the natural sciences, the social sciences, and the humanities. This sort of generic WAC is, as Williams says, a compromise. It cannot provide the rich context of a link, but it can alert students to issues of perspective and help them learn to read critically. The links have also had a subtle effect on basic pedagogy. The general composition courses now incorporate more individual conferences between teachers and students, and encourage students to make more holistic evaluations of each other's written work: The model for these readily adaptable activities has been the writing links (Lindemann).

The wider influence of link course practices has become evident at the University of Washington too, although such influence took longer to develop. That is partly because what is now one of the oldest, largest link course programs began very small and grew slowly for several years before there was much contact between writing link teachers and those teaching traditional freshman composition.

The UW program originated in a series of conversations between a writing teacher and a historian in 1975. Both were frustrated, for it seemed that an opportunity for powerful teaching lay between them, and neither could reach it. They decided that linking courses would be worth a try. But the writing teacher would have to go into the context created by a *large* history lecture course to find a pool of students from which to draw a writing course enrollment, because the link would be optional, a modest experiment in course design.

That first experiment was highly instructive: It made clear, for example, that in a well-defined, resource-rich context for writing, one should make just a few paper assignments and cultivate the thinking called for by each, rather than moving rapidly from one paper assignment to the next as was common then in freestanding composition courses. The link situation made conferences exceptionally productive, and students responded in very practical ways to each other's work. Also, class time could be well used: There was no need to spend it motivating students or making assignments credible, and lecture course readings would reward, for writing instruction purposes, much more examination than they got in the lecture course itself. Lines between reading, writing, and critical thinking tended to disappear.

So more experiments were made, involving a few more writing teachers and a few more discipline lecturers. Writing teachers were paid through the Office for Undergraduate Studies, a now-extinct administrative unit that supported curriculum innovations. The links brought logistical problems, and course design problems too— but the opportunities they offered were overwhelmingly attractive. So program development was pursued, and with the help of a 1977-79 grant from the Fund for Improvement of Secondary Education (FIPSE), a pattern of offerings was regularized. The link course program, known at the UW as the Interdisciplinary Writing Program (IWP), functioned as an independent administrative entity under the dean of the College of Arts and Sciences until 1984, then became a semiautonomous operation within the Department of English.

This institutionalizing move has brought increased interaction between administrators and teachers in the freshman composition program and those in the IWP. Virtually all teachers in the traditional program continue to be TAs, however, while the IWP has seven core faculty members—people hired specifically for IWP work. In addition, four English TAs with experience in the traditional program now hold IWP appointments each year: They are selected for two-year, staggered terms. And TAs from other disciplines are taking an increasing part. Some departments have recently received extra TA appointments for graduate students to teach writing links; those graduate students join IWP core faculty experienced in their discipline for small course-development seminars during the first quarter in which they teach.

All new IWP teachers, whether TAs or core faculty, from English or from other disciplines, take part in a week-long fall workshop before the term begins. This common experience is essential because links put writing teachers in a situation that in one way or another is new for all. The workshop concentrates on two major issues: How to develop a writing course that is constantly responsive to, constantly capitalizing on, its context and how to play a link teacher's role.

Both issues have to be considered in terms of the UW's particular kind of link program. Except for a few honors links, all IWP courses accompany general education lecture courses, some of which are also relevant to majors; the lecture courses all have very large enrollments—from 100 to 500 students. A given lecture class might be accompanied by one to four link classes of 20 students each. Except in the Honors Program, links are always optional, but they are a popular way to satisfy writing requirements. In 1991-92, the IWP offered 22 to 24 classes each quarter: About 1,500 students took writing links during the year.

Many of the lecture courses accompanied by links require one or two papers of some kind, and lecture course writing assignments become joint assignments—required in the links as well. Additional major assignments as well as many smaller assignments must be designed for link students. The primary text for link classes is the writing that students produce; links also make use of lecture course readings for rhetorical and critical analysis, and may employ additional, brief readings from the discipline.

If, for example, a lecture course assigns only an introductory textbook, students will need to see something of how textbook statements were arrived at, how methods of investigation are related to conclusions, perhaps how different theories might be evaluated as explanations in a given case. If a lecture course assigns primary documents, say the diaries of colonists or Vietnam veterans, the problems and opportunities implicit in readings will be quite different. If a lecture course assigns independent library research, on the basis of which students must formulate causal questions about events— reading/writing activities will be different again. Writing link students are encouraged to identify the functions of statements in readings and lectures and to see disciplines as sites of ongoing investigations and arguments. Designing exploratory and analytical activities for link students makes a considerable demand on writing teachers.

However, as the above may suggest, lecture courses at the UW are not necessarily changed at all by the presence of writing links. Sometimes faculty planning sessions and/or interactions between link teachers and discussion section TAs *do* bring changes, but this occurs only as individual personalities and circumstances permit. Regardless of the degree to which link teachers act as consultants, they must be prepared to learn themselves from lecture contexts, increasing their understanding of disciplinary perspectives and watching for ways to employ lecture course problems and strategies for their own teaching purpose.

Several of the points Chris Thaiss makes (this volume) about the nature of general education courses are highly relevant to link teachers' opportunities and roles. For one thing, because the goals of general education courses tend to be broad, they offer much room for experiment with writing assignments. Making writing instruction available in general education contexts is particularly important too, for as Thaiss points out, beginning students often lack confidence, and they know little about the discourse communities they are entering. Also they often assume that compiling and reciting facts is all they need to do, and large lectures easily encourage a passive, alienated stance. Furthermore, because students may enroll in general education courses simply to fulfill requirements, they may not reflect on what they learn or try to connect course learning to anything else in their experience. Fragmentation both within courses and between courses is all too often what is expected, and also what results.

Writing links help change this situation. By offering writing instruction in the context of students' study, they promote active engagement and the integration of learning. IWP teachers identify in certain ways with their students' experience, and in their classrooms they often play a sort of master-learner role. Legitimizing and helping to refine students' questions, at times exposing their own uncertainties and working with students to identify alternatives, they teach partly by modeling engagement in inquiry. It usually takes a little time to become comfortable in a link teacher's role. While experienced writing teachers may be accustomed to enacting more than presenting their expertise—crucial for IWP work—they must learn to exploit an unfolding context that they don't themselves create. Also because they adopt discipline-bound writing purposes and deal directly with issues on which they are not expert, they may feel their authority is jeopardized. But the context is always in some way highly stimulating: Authority anxiety tends to disappear as teachers realize how much they can see that their students, at the outset, cannot—and so identify ways that the context can further writing teachers' aims.

ASSUMPTIONS AND PITFALLS OF INTEGRATED WRITING PROGRAMS

The pitfalls for integrated writing instruction are inseparable from the opportunities. Vulnerability to some pitfalls—or limitations, at least—is a necessary condition for some of the most productive program designs. I will list here some assumptions made by all programs, then compare some key program features to identify the advantages that particular models present.

Assumptions Made by All Integrated Writing Programs

1. The relationship between a lecture and a writing component, adjunct, or link does not represent a split between content and form. In fact, components and links are especially powerful ways to work *against* such a split. It is in order to work against it that, for example, writing instructors commonly sit in on the lectures their students take. Adjuncts are more vulnerable to being perceived as form focused, because they provide so little teaching time, but that is why adjuncts tend eventually either to disappear from a curriculum or to become something more—i.e., components or links.

2. Faculty and graduate students in English can provide valuable writing instruction for students in the disciplines—if they go to the disciplinary contexts where students are working and expect to learn

themselves. Graduate students in the disciplines can also provide valuable writing instruction for students, given appropriate opportunity to learn about writing.

3. What students learn in a given component, adjunct, or link is obviously in some ways context bound—one does not learn to write once and for all, and generic "good writing" is a problematic concept. On the other hand, writing instruction for students immersed in a context does have some carrying power. Most notably, students learn what to look for, how to recognize things that matter when they go to contexts that are new.

Key Features of Integrated Writing Programs: Summary Comparisons

Inclusiveness. The UC San Diego program—a sequence of core lecture courses with writing components—includes all freshmen. Such a plan provides "a common intellectual experience," and it is feasible in UC San Diego's Third College, given that an entering class is about 600 students. It would also be feasible in many other effectively small-college situations, but it probably would not be in large institutions with freshman classes of several thousand.

The North Carolina program at Chapel Hill—several semester-long, especially designed lecture courses accompanied by writing links—will accommodate only a small fraction of the freshman class. But this is an inclusive program in the sense that all the students taking a given lecture course are also enrolled in links.

The adjunct programs at UCLA and UC Santa Barbara and the link programs at UC Davis and at UW are not inclusive in either sense. The adjuncts and links are optional companions to lecture courses, so some lecture course students take writing concurrently but others do not. Lectures are not developed specifically for these programs; the bond between lectures and writing classes is, therefore, not as tight. The advantage of the looser noninclusive structure is flexibility. Links can be arranged with relative ease and can be offered with a wide range of disciplines.

Levels and Special Student Populations. As noted above, the UC San Diego and UNC Chapel Hill programs are exclusively for freshmen. The UC Davis program is for upper-division students, who must already have satisfied a lower-division writing requirement. The adjuncts at UC Santa Barbara and UCLA have also been largely for upper-division students, but UC Santa Barbara is making basic changes in its program, and UCLA uses integrated writing instruction in situations other than upper-division adjuncts. These include a long-standing summer transition program for at-risk students, and a new, year-long program that encourages at-risk students to choose education as a professional field. UCLA is also now offering links in a program for upper-division transfer students.

The UW writing links accompany general education courses in many disciplines at the freshman and sophomore level. Overall, about two-thirds of the students who take the UW links are freshmen, but a given class might have mostly sophomores because of the level of the lecture course it accompanies. Students in the Arts and Sciences Honors Program have long been required to take a writing link with one of their core courses, and that pattern has helped break down the once very common faculty assumption that writing courses were essentially remedial work.

Lecture Course Selection. Where lectures are chosen for adjuncts or links rather than created as program constituents, some care must be taken—and of course there will still be surprises. It is often useful to talk early with the member of a department's staff who handles course scheduling: That person will usually know which courses are of an appropriate size, when and how regularly they will be offered, who commonly teaches them, and perhaps something of teachers' interests and styles. The chair of a department's undergraduate curriculum committee may also be a good source of information, but once basic inquiries have been made, it is important for program developers to talk personally with faculty whose courses may be appropriate for links. Of course, such faculty may also seek out a program developer to offer a course and request links, once the possibility becomes known.

In any case, lectures chosen for links should usually be those that students perceive as somewhat demanding. It is an important advantage if a course emphasizes issues or problems, not just mastery of facts (which is why, among general education courses, one called "Introduction to . . ." may be better than one called "Survey of . . ."). It is a further advantage if the discipline lecturer discusses in class some of her discipline's methods of inquiry, and models the kinds of investigation and analysis that students should engage in by occasionally incorporating them in lecture presentations. The prospect for these things may not be possible to predict, but it may well be possible to encourage.

So far as writing requirements go, the link bond is tighter, of course, if at least one assignment is being made in the lecture course, and that assignment becomes joint, i.e., is required in the link course as well. At the UW, at least three-quarters of the lectures accompanied by links do make writing assignments; the rest have links because the perspectives and materials and issues they present make such good writing occasions and because the lecturers are happy to consult with writing link teachers.

Sometimes is necessary to assure faculty who offer large lectures that writing links will not make sizable new demands on them. (If a program developer does not wish to make such assurances, the pool of appropriate lectures will obviously be smaller.) It is partly because links can operate without the contribution of much discipline faculty time that they are so valuable in large, research-oriented institutions, where such time is almost never available. There are just a few essentials: Lecturers must have a conversation or two with link teachers before a term begins so that calendars can be coordinated, and lecture course purposes and readings as well as any joint writing assignments can be discussed. Beyond that, link teachers should find out whether lecturers will have weekly meetings with TAs who lead discussion sections and ask to sit in on such meetings if they are held. Probably nothing more will be necessary, although at some point a link teacher might need to seek a discipline lecturer's reaction or advice on her plans for a link course assignment.

There is, of course, much opportunity beyond what is essential, and link teachers need to respond to whatever the situation provides. It may turn out that discussion section TAs are a very important resource, for they see much more of students than discipline lecturers do, and they may have more inclination to talk over teaching questions. Or it may turn out that a discipline lecturer eagerly seeks writing link teachers' participation in TA training sessions he conducts, and a strongly interacting group is formed. Some relationships will be distant, others close: When lecture courses are chosen from existing offerings rather than created for the program's purpose, writing teachers must live with that.

Staffing Writing Components, Adjuncts, and Links. Two points need to be made:

A. Teachers cannot simply be assigned to classes in integrated writing programs. Some English TAs who take graduate degrees in English will be uncomfortable—feel themselves cramped or compromised—if they must take other disciplines' writing purposes seriously. Other people flourish. Similarly, some teachers in the disciplines are impatient with writing concerns and interact poorly with students. Others are terrific. Teachers in integrated writing programs must be *selected,* and the selection should be based on interviews as well as documents.

B. In programs where lectures are created for the purpose of integration with writing instruction, an all-TA staff for writing components or links is practical (see the discussion of UC San Diego and UNC Chapel Hill). Because there are just a few lecture courses to be dealt with, because lecturers are active and concerned participants in program design, and because teachers with related tasks think of themselves as teams, this staffing pattern can work.

However, where lectures are not created for programs and many different, somewhat unpredictable lecture courses are involved, an integrated writing program must have core faculty—faculty committed to teaching writing, interested in course development, and prepared to practice discourse analysis on the fly.

Both situations and staffing patterns have advantages. In the first case, the strong interaction among lecturers, writing directors, and TAs is likely to produce excellent classes for students as well as satisfying experience for teachers—but the participants are relatively few. In the second case, there is much less concentrated, immediate interaction for teachers, but a much wider exposure of opportunities. In so far as optional writing adjuncts and links are arranged across the curriculum, there is the possibility of wide influence among discipline faculty. There is also a great (almost overwhelming) amount of stimulating experience in disciplinary discourse communities for faculty on the writing side. UW link teachers have found themselves engaged not only in consultation on teaching issues but in analysis of texts produced by their lecturing colleagues, trying to understand, say, the changes made as an article goes from reader to reader and draft to draft. Of course, this doesn't happen all the time, but professional relationships do form, and friendships as well.

TRAINING AND SUPPORT FOR TEACHERS
IN INTEGRATED WRITING PROGRAMS

Even for experienced writing teachers some preliminary meetings to explore the implications of context-bound work are important. Contexts offer a great deal to writing teachers, but they often require them to use materials that are new, to think about writing purposes in new ways, to interact with discipline faculty in new ways, and to play a somewhat altered classroom role. Interaction among writing teachers as courses go forward is also valuable for all, but it is essential for writing teachers who are not experienced. Because in integrated writing programs TAs from the disciplines often do some teaching, this matter needs special attention. Perhaps the most common assumption of those who have not taught writing before is that, in class, their primary job will be to present information about writing. When it becomes clear that information *about* writing does not necessarily help students engage *in* writing to good result, they may become very worried about how class time should be spent. They need consultation opportunities while they are teaching, and of course their consultant can expect to learn from them as well, for they are further inside their discipline's perspective.

Increased interaction between discipline TAs and writing faculty who teach links at the UW is being planned as more TAs come into the program. Small seminars during TAs' first quarter of teaching are new. First experiments have involved IWP faculty members experienced with lecture courses in art history and political science, and three to four TAs from each discipline; all members of each seminar concurrently teach writing links.

SCHEDULING AND PUBLICITY

For a program using components, scheduling must take into account the extra time required for a course carrying more than the usual amount of credit. For programs with adjuncts or links, writing courses and lecture courses are usually scheduled separately and by different departments. Good exchange of scheduling information is necessary, and it may be important to include cross-references between writing and lecture courses in students' registration materials. As for times selected for adjuncts and links, the key consideration may be whether they are required or not. Scheduling is flexible when such courses are required, as in the program at UNC Chapel Hill. That program's lecture courses meet in the morning, but the links are in the afternoon when classrooms are easy to find and when other, somewhat analogous courses (like laboratories that accompany science courses) meet. At the UW, however, most links are optional, so they must be scheduled to accommodate students who often work and/or commute. For that reason, UW links are usually the hour after or the hour before the lecture they accompany.

Beyond attention to scheduling and clear registration information, publicity about new offerings may be important. Students usually have had no experience with integrated writing instruction, so they do not anticipate it. Experiments with optional, integrated writing instruction have been made at various schools over the years, but they remained isolated instances either because they were perceived as a passing interest of eccentric faculty or because there seemed to be little student demand. Simply announcing when a term begins that writing adjuncts or links are available is not adequate: Students need to know what such courses are.

UNC Chapel Hill did such a good job of explaining new writing links in its brochure for incoming freshmen that course requests came in a flood. At the UW the program is larger and less compact; links accompany many different lecture courses and they are not exclusively for freshmen, so publicity has been more complicated. Also, the UW's links were, for several years, listed as general studies courses rather than as English courses, so students looking for writing instruction often did not find them in registration schedules. Enrollment then depended a lot on first-day announcements and information distributed in lecture classes where links were attached. But that method is rarely needed now. Links have been listed under "English" since 1984, so they are readily found; links have acquired a strong reputation; and academic advisors—both in the Central Advising Office and in departments—make the links known.

INFLUENCES OF INTEGRATED WRITING
INSTRUCTION ON DISCIPLINE LECTURES

Beyond the construction of lecture courses for program purposes, existing lectures are often influenced by writing adjuncts or links. Such influence may be subtle, a matter of gradually changing faculty assumptions about writing and learning. Or it may be quite obvious, as when a lecturer changes the language of writing assignments, makes more or different assignments, requires drafts, holds paper-reading sessions with TAs, and so on. Whether, or how much, writing teachers in adjuncts or links should try to influence lecture courses must be decided with due regard for interacting factors in each case.

At UCLA, part of the purpose of adjuncts has been to influence lecture courses. Adjunct teachers have served as writing consultants. In many respects the result has been good—important changes have been made. But there is one important difficulty: The workload of TAs who lead discussion sections is usually increased by changes related to writing—when, for example, they must respond to students' drafts. If the number of students assigned to each TA is not reduced, TAs may resent changes, even undermine them.

At UW, although link teachers have certainly been influential in some cases, there has been no programmatic attempt to provoke change in lecture courses by having link teachers serve as consultants. This, in many ways, is wasteful. Writing teachers whose own work has brought them into disciplinary contexts are unusually well qualified to play a consulting role. One promising development is that more attention is now being given to TA training across the institution. It is possible that some departments will begin using their large lecture courses more deliberately as occasions for such training. If that happens, consultant roles for writing link teachers will almost inevitably be strengthened, for the large lecture courses with many TAs are the very courses that have links. The prospect for lecture course improvement by focusing on TA training is very attractive, but UW will have to be wary of the workload issues that have emerged at UCLA.

INFLUENCES OF INTEGRATED WRITING
INSTRUCTION ON TRADITIONAL COMPOSITION

Changed designs for general composition courses are sometimes clearly responses to the WAC movement, as is the case with the Yale course Linda Peterson describes in this volume. But forces that generated the WAC movement have also been expressed in writing components, adjuncts, and links—and such innovations have become influences in themselves.

As noted above, at UNC Chapel Hill and at UW link examples have helped make conferences on drafts a more significant part of general composition teaching; also the link practice of focusing on students' drafts as whole pieces of purpose-directed work has encouraged general composition teachers to move students engaged in peer review away from a piecemeal style of response. Increased significance of conferencing and more holistic responses to drafts—these changes result from and help to create a renewed respect for the difficulty of students' tasks, and for the texts they produce. Stress on the powerful connections between writing and learning has helped renew interest in what teachers can learn from students' texts—and it has helped weaken the idea that generic good writing, regardless of purpose, can exist. Eventually integrated writing instruction may even help relate personal values achieved by writing to social contexts in which writers work, because integrated instruction reveals students' capacity to be personally engaged even as they produce discourse that is academic.

WORKS CITED

Cooper, Charles. Telephone interview. July 1990; Jan. 1992.

Cullen, Robert J. "Writing Across the Curriculum: Adjunct Courses." *ADE Bulletin* 80 (Spring 1985): 15-17.

Hilgers, Thomas L., and Joy Marsella. *Making Your Writing Program Work: A Guide to Good Practices*. Newbury Park, CA: Sage, 1992.

Lindemann, Erika. Telephone interview. May 1990.

MacDonald, Susan Peck. Telephone interview. June 1990; Jan. 1992.

Palo, Susan. Telephone interview. June 1990; Jan. 1992.

Strenski, Ellen. Telephone interview. May 1990; Jan. 1992.

Williams, Jim. Telephone interview. Jan. 1992.

Zimmerman, Muriel. Telephone interview. June 1990; Jan. 1992.

NINE

The Writing Consultant
Collaboration and Team Teaching

PESHE C. KURILOFF

Both the philosophy and structure of writing across the curriculum make collaboration a natural outcome. Collaboration among students through the peer review process in courses and through writing fellows programs like that at Brown University (which is described in this volume), has received considerable attention. The positive effects of students helping students are well documented.

A less publicized but equally valuable aspect of writing across the curriculum involves collaboration among teachers. In many cases "the writing consultant," often the WAC administrator, responds to faculty or administrative interest in teaching writing in disciplinary courses. As the writing expert, the consultant brings knowledge of the writing process and pedagogy to the interaction, but such expertise is not sufficient to ensure that students learn to write psychology or history. The professor of anthropology, for example, must learn about drafting and revising, but the writing consultant must also learn about the conventions of anthropology. Successful outcomes depend on an exchange of information and ideas between two experts, the writing consultant and the content area instructor.

Nearly every program featured in a recent book subtitled *Models and Methods for Writing Across the Curriculum* (Fulwiler and Young) depends at least in part for its success on collaboration among writing consultants and nonwriting teachers. Although this collaboration typically involves faculty from different departments or even different schools working together on a writing committee, or experienced writing instructors consulting with nonwriting faculty teaching writing-intensive courses, more intimate arrangements not infrequently occur. As the Baltimore Area Consortium has documented (McCarthy and Walvoord), collaborators in writing across the curriculum sometimes undertake research together. In other cases, faculty from different disciplines work as a team, creating new courses and teaching them collaboratively. In this chapter, I present one model of consultation that involves collaborative course design and team teaching.

THEORETICAL FRAMEWORK

The rationale for the type of collaboration I present rests on a few theoretical assumptions generally associated with writing across the curriculum. The first specifies the existence of discourse communities (see Bizzell), often linked to disciplinary communities to which students seek, through reading and writing, access. The reality of these different discourse communities within the larger academic community, each with its own distinctive conventions, makes the need for collaboration among insiders in various communities imperative. Obviously, outsiders cannot effectively prepare students for entry into a community to which they themselves do not belong. Only by learning about each other's communities can teachers help ease the transitions for students as they learn about writing, not once and for all, but repeatedly as they take courses across the curriculum and are exposed to the variety of conventions and practices that characterize writing in different fields and in different courses within those fields (Jolliffe and Brier).

James Kinneavy divides the theoretical foundations for WAC into two dimensions: the dimension of audience and that of functions of language. The audience dimension he affiliates with concern about discourse communities. This school of WAC, Kinneavy suggests, focuses on teaching student writers how to join the ongoing conversation of their disciplines. He associates the second dimension with writing to learn. Practitioners cite the need to encourage students to use writing as a tool for learning (and creating knowledge) and less as a means of relaying existing knowledge. These WAC courses use journals; freewriting; and responses to discussion, lectures, and readings to accomplish their goals. These distinctions have been reviewed by McLeod (this volume).

Again, as numerous researchers have demonstrated (e.g., Faigley and Hansen), teaching students to use writing as a tool for learning requires knowledge about the subject being learned to which writing instructors on their own do not have access. Only as a result of collaboration can writing instructors and so-called content instructors work together to create assignments, develop criteria for evaluation, and help students realize the intimate relationship that exists between thinking and writing in any field.

In addition to emphasizing the need to socialize students into discourse communities and the role of writing in learning, many WAC instructors see critical reading (often defined as critical thinking) and writing as closely allied. Students learn to write in the context of learning the discourse of the discipline, which is communicated to them largely through readings. Learning to read intelligently, with a critical eye to the conventions being observed and their role in both creating and communicating knowledge, is an essential tool for students seeking mastery over a particular type of discourse. All writers depend on appropriate models when making choices about their own texts. The processes of deciding on appropriate models and identifying critical reading strategies proceed more smoothly in a collaborative environment. With a writing instructor asking the right questions and a content instructor proposing answers, both teachers learn more than they could possibly discover alone.

THE PROCESS OF COLLABORATION:
A WORKING MODEL

With such strong reasons supporting collaborative course design and team teaching, why not incorporate both as clearly desirable features of WAC? Time and money spring immediately to mind as forces working against collaboration. The process of collaboration takes precious time from professionals in a highly labor-intensive field, professionals who already need more time than they can give for their students; and team teaching, unless responsibilities are carefully defined so that each instructor teaches only half the course, can rapidly drain a program's resources. To work effectively, to the benefit of both teachers and students, collaboration needs to be carefully structured. A description of one model that was developed by a team of instructors at the University of Pennsylvania can serve as a model (see Figure 9.1).[1]

As a result of student initiative, as well as administrative and faculty concern about students' communication skills, the School of Engineering and Applied Science at the University of Pennsylvania decided to develop an upper-level communications course designed for third-year students in all departments of the engineering school. Because Writing Across the University (WATU), Penn's WAC program, enjoyed a good working relationship with engineering, WATU was called in to consult and eventually asked to direct the project. Funds were provided to support two graduate assistants in English to research programs across the country and gather resources as well as, and most important, to provide release time for a senior professor in engineering to work with me, the director of WATU, as part of a team. This relationship proved fruitful, and we have now offered the course, taught first by the graduate students/research assistants and then by me, repeatedly and successfully as part of the engineering curriculum. In addition, I worked collaboratively with an assistant professor in the nursing school on a similar course for nursing students, which we team taught the first semester and then the nursing professor taught herself. (Syllabi for both courses appear in the Appendix to this chapter.) Details of both experiences follow.

Stage 1: Joint Goal Setting

Our initial team meetings were devoted to understanding each other's interests, primarily those of the engineering faculty and those of the writing instructors, and identifying goals and the means to achieve those goals on which we could agree. We decided immediately to avoid the constraints of so-called technical writing courses and to aim for a high level of proficiency comparable with what we would expect of any student in the university. The following questions guided our discussions:

A. Stage 1: Joint Goal Setting
   1. What is the relationship between reading and writing?
   2. What should students learn about each?
   3. What kinds of reading and writing should they do?
   4. How should we evaluate students' progress?
   5. What type of classroom environment should we foster?
B. Stage 2: Inquiry and Self-Study
   1. What are the forms of writing used in this discipline?
   2. What do these forms reveal about how practitioners think?
   3. How is new knowledge created?
   4. What type of reasoning, what type of questions, what type of evidence does this discipline respect?
   5. What kind of language is used?
C. Stage 3: Creating a Context
   1. What forms of writing are appropriate for student writers?
   2. What audiences should they address?
   3. What purposes should they achieve?
   4. What models should they read?
   5. How do we want students to think?
   6. What is their relationship to knowledge inside their field and outside it?
D. Stage 4: Implementation
   1. What will the writing assignments be?
   2. What texts will we assign?
   3. How will we emphasize the writing process?
   4. In what ways can we combine writing and thinking activities?
E. Stage 5: Evaluation
   1. How will we define success?
   2. What feedback do we want?
   3. How can we best acquire that feedback?

Figure 9.1 A Collaborative Model for Creating Writing Across the Curriculum Courses

1. What relationship should be established between reading and writing?
2. What should students learn about each?
3. What kinds of reading and writing should students do?
4. How should they be evaluated?
5. What type of classroom environment should be fostered?

Answering these questions required some negotiation, but no major obstacles appeared. We agreed that because reading and writing are best taught in conjunction we would offer readings that could serve as models for the various ways writers could address technical subjects. We also wanted to create a course both students and faculty could enjoy. We believed it was particularly important for engineering students to emerge from the course with a positive attitude about communication skills and self-confidence about their ability to communicate effectively. We agreed that students should become comfortable with the writing process, that they should write about technical subjects with which they were familiar, and that they should gain experience with the forms of writing they would encounter as professionals. As part of this endeavor, we also agreed that we wanted students to learn how the values and assumptions about knowledge are transmitted in the forms of writing practiced in their discipline, along with how the purpose of a piece of writing influences its form and style, and how the audience with which they intend to communicate guides decision making at all stages of the writing process.

To provide students with experience communicating with an audience, we decided to create a community of readers and writers in the class who would routinely work collaboratively, read each other's writing, and offer feedback. We hoped in this way to avoid the problem of students writing exclusively for an instructor whose background and interests might be quite different from theirs. To promote independence and help them develop good judgment, we also wanted students to evaluate their success as writers based on the feedback received from their peers rather than the grade assigned by the teacher.

So much common ground is not easily established, but some common ground is mandatory for a collaborative venture of this sort to succeed. I found that, although we used different words to express it, we had similar goals for our students. By raising the same questions I would raise in any writing situation, we were able to identify our priorities and to reach a common understanding about how issues of form, audience, purpose, and the relationship between reading and writing would be handled in the course. The specific answers to questions such as "What audiences should students address?" came later, after a period of self-discovery and learning about each other's ways of thinking. By this point, however, we had established some common goals that paved the way for the next stage.

Stage 2: Inquiry and Self-Study

In the most typical forms of WAC consultation among faculty, writing instructors try to initiate nonwriting faculty into the mysteries of teaching writing. In some cases, however, and definitely in this one, both participants educate each other. Although simply hearing about the field of engineering proved stimulating, a guided inquiry, centering on some carefully identified questions, elicited the information I needed to know to be able to make suggestions about the writing component of the course:

1. What are the forms of writing practiced in engineering?
2. What do those forms reveal about how engineers think?
3. How is new knowledge created?
4. What type of reasoning, what type of questions, what type of evidence do engineers respect?
5. What type of language do they use?

This process of inquiry produced interesting results, one of which was a theme for the course, the theme of building, later modified to the theme of problem solving, both metaphors for writing with which we thought engineers could readily identify. The questions themselves led to profitable discussions about the role of writing in the engineering profession and in academic engineering, which were enriched by readings in composition research related to teaching technical writing. They also helped to reveal the intellectual foundation in composition theory that I used to structure the inquiry. By addressing these questions, we eliminated any temptation to rely on the surface features of writing to create a shared vocabulary or to identify common interests. My collaborator from engineering became engaged in the intricacies of discourse as I absorbed the premises of engineering. Once we were comfortable with each other's habits of mind, making joint decisions about the content of the course seemed almost inevitable.

Stage 3: Creating a Context

Learning about engineering discourse was a prerequisite for understanding how students might relate to that discourse. Sensitive to the problems Herrington cites in her description of two engineering classes, we wanted to create as appropriate and realistic a context for student writing as we could.

To help ourselves translate the results of our inquiry into a classroom context, we raised the following questions:

1. How do we want engineering students to think?
2. What is their relationship to knowledge in their field and outside it?
3. What forms and styles of writing are appropriate for them to practice?
4. What audiences should they address?
5. What purposes should they consider?
6. What texts can serve as models for them?

Recognizing that their status as students defined their relationship to their discourse community, we knew that we could not expect them to read and write like professional engineers. In fact, we were not sure such a goal was even desirable. We wanted them to learn to write like engineers, but we also wanted them to learn to write like their peers across the university. My collaborator in engineering represented the needs of his discourse community toward which we wanted to encourage students to move; and my function as the writing specialist became that of ensuring that engineering students, like any students I might teach, learn what I could teach them about the cognitive processes that inform writing (e.g., planning and goal setting), including how to write for diverse purposes and meet the needs of a variety of audiences. After some investigation, we determined that engineering students wrote primarily lab reports and technical reports for their instructors until their senior design projects, which were written for professionals. Only as seniors did they have an opportunity to influence an audience actively or to make claims of their own. We wanted to correct this situation. At the same time, we wanted to recognize the significance of effective communication with audiences, like professors, with whom they were already familiar. Our concerns about critical thinking and writing led us to the same conclusions. As we answered the questions we had posed, the concrete features of our curriculum emerged. We decided that:

1. Students should learn to define, describe, inform, report, instruct, and propose. They should also learn to generate purposes of their own, to recognize that a variety of needs might be served through written communication, and to use writing along with other tools, particularly their refined visual thinking skills, to enhance learning.

2. Students should write lab reports/technical reports, instructions, proposals, and descriptions as well as become acquainted with more open-ended forms of writing, primarily the essay.

3. They should write for their current discourse community (other engineering students), their future discourse community (professional engineers), their peers across the university, and themselves.

4. They should learn to write the professional style of choice and also a more informal style appropriate for nonengineers as well as an informal academic style similar to that required of students in arts and sciences. They should learn about the conventions of their disciplines and about those that govern other disciplines or define other discourse communities to which they might at some point wish to gain access (such as the community of well-informed citizens).

5. They should become familiar with all stages of the writing process, with a special emphasis on planning, which seemed compatible with their usual approach to problem solving. They should have opportunities to practice those stages with feedback from all members of the classroom community, not just the instructor.

6. Many models exist with which they are not familiar. We sought historical, technical documents to help them achieve some perspective on their own discourse community, well-written technical documents, and a variety of writings about technical subjects that we felt they might reasonably aspire to write some day. We developed long lists of documentary works, novels, books of poetry, academic studies as well as examples of more conventional technical writing.

Stage 4: Implementation

Once the conceptual work was done, implementation proceeded smoothly. We decided on four major writing assignments: a lab/technical report, a set of instructions, a proposal, and an essay. In each case, students were to use their knowledge and perspective as engineers to inform their writing. We planned to require drafts of each of these four assignments. In between the longer assignments we created shorter, informal assignments, such as a problem definition, a problem solution, and a brief nontechnical report written for a lay audience.

We discussed in detail how to articulate these assignments and ensure that they met established engineering standards as well as standards of common discourse. The lab report proved the most problematic to pin down. We thought about creating a minilaboratory in class, using a paper clip experiment, but eventually my colleague in engineering proposed to contribute a computer-simulated design experiment, which the students could use as the subject of their technical reports. We defined the problem in a way that would allow students to recommend any one of three possible solutions, depending on how they used the data. As a result, we would be able to concentrate on the rhetoric of the report rather than the accuracy of the "solution."

Other collaborative assignments included readings of historical, technical documents (supplied by our engineer) to give students some idea of the development of technical communication. (The prose in older, technical documents tends to be much more literary than that used by engineers today.) By mutual agreement we used *Zen and the Art of Motorcycle Maintenance* as the foundation reading for the instructions assignment, and Alan Trachtenberg's *Brooklyn Bridge: Fact and Symbol,* an account of the building of the Brooklyn Bridge written by a professor of American studies that emphasizes the bridge's role as a cultural symbol.

Because team teaching was not an option in this first collaborative venture, we worked out procedures for cooperation and support. Our representative engineer would be available to consult with students and the instructors on the technical aspects of the work for the class and would visit periodically to reinforce the notion that the course, identified as a humanities elective, also had validity from the perspective of engineering.

Stage 5: Evaluation

We developed a questionnaire for students and spent the last class evaluating the course; both my colleague in engineering and I read sample papers in an effort to determine whether the goals we had established for the course were met. After the course had been taught a few times, we hired an outside evaluator to gain additional perspective and to enable us to provide the dean, who had financed our efforts, with some external evidence of accomplishment. A suggestion by the evaluator led us to restructure the course somewhat, but the basic format, guided by the same objectives, has persisted over quite a few years.

REPLICATING THE RESULTS

Our success in engineering aroused interest in another professional school and led us to clone the class for nursing students. The same process of collaboration guided our decisions about writing activities and readings, although this time we had a model, which made the process much simpler. As a result of our inquiry into nursing practice and discussion of what we might expect of nursing students, we chose to keep the theme of problem solving and most of the writing activities, varying the readings and the parameters of the assignments to make them more appropriate for and more interesting to nursing students. We added writing activities like case notes, a routine writing activity for nurses, and changed the instructions into a health care brochure. We also added readings such as Susan Sontag's *Illness as Metaphor*, to broaden the students' perspective on health and illness, and sample case referrals to provide examples of writing in professional practice. We substituted an account by a consumer of the health care system for the Trachtenberg book. In spite of these differences, the courses had more in common than not. Probably the most significant difference resulted from the additional funding that allowed us to team teach the nursing course.

TEAM TEACHING

Establishing Common Goals

Probably the most important issue in team teaching is compatibility, which enables the team to establish common goals. To work effectively together, both instructors must feel secure and each must respect and value the other's expertise. The process of designing the course and setting goals offers a reasonable test of compatibility. If possible, it's a good idea to withhold a decision about team teaching until the design process is near completion. The specific arrangement you work out will depend a great deal on what you learn about each other as you gain experience working together (see Figure 9.2). I have found faculty who volunteer for collaborative projects generally make comfortable teammates. This case was no exception.

Assigning Responsibilities and Defining Roles

Teams made up of content instructors and writing instructors are common in WAC programs, but these teams infrequently work together in the same classroom. Determining who takes responsibility for what in a subject matter-based writing course can raise difficult questions about the relationship between the content of a text and its expression.

In the case of the nursing class, our roles tended to define themselves naturally in relation to our respective areas of expertise. We agreed that we should both attend class as much as possible, but that one of us would act as primary instructor each time. It seemed sensible for me to teach those classes that focused on the writing process, critical reading, and peer review. My colleague in nursing took responsibility for discussing the readings, explaining formats, and interpreting the discourse conventions of nursing. Because our roles sometimes overlapped (learning how to read critically also involved discussing an article), we simply

1. Establishing common goals.

   Reach consensus on the purposes and aims of the course.

   Decide how reading and writing will interact.

   Determine the type of classroom environment you want to create.

2. Assigning responsibilities.

   Identify tasks and divide them as equitably as possible between you.

   Ensure that someone is in charge of each class.

   Determine how often each of you will attend class and who will read each assignment.

   Decide who will teach what material.

3. Defining roles.

   Clarify each instructor's status in the classroom.

   Make sure students understand the relationship between you.

   Identify roles with which each instructor feels comfortable.

   Ensure that writing instructor is not reduced to grammarian or stylist.

   Clarify relationship of each instructor to each assignment.

   Use differences in perspective as material for the course.

4. Establishing evaluation procedures.

   Establish procedures for evaluation jointly.

   Separate evaluation procedures from judgments about quality of writing.

   Ensure that both instructors have equal status as evaluators.

Figure 9.2 A Model for Team Teaching WAC Courses

took turns or contributed our individual perspectives as appropriate. The differences in how, for example, we read a text created valuable discussion about audience and how discourse conventions work to include targeted readers and exclude outsiders.

Establishing Evaluation Procedures

The same issues arose in relation to response to writing. Students always received feedback from both of us (as well as from each other). Depending on the identified audience for a paper, we took turns playing the role of primary reader. Students learned that because we brought our individual interests to our reading they needed to decide whose concerns they should respond to first. Not infrequently, we attended to different aspects of their writing. For the health care brochure, for example, the nursing instructor focused on the accuracy and appropriateness of the information provided, whereas I was concerned primarily with my ability to learn from and be influenced by the material. Because of our different perspectives, evaluation could have posed a problem. Our earlier decision to refrain from grading the weekly assignments and use portfolio assessment to evaluate the students made the process much smoother. Because we had been careful to articulate our goals before we began, by the end of the semester, we found our views of student work and progress quite similar. The grades students received depended not on whether we thought a paper was good but on how well the student had accomplished the goals for the course, goals such as learning about the conventions of writing in nursing and learning to meet the needs of the intended audience.

THE RISKS OF COLLABORATION

The examples just described worked well in our particular context, but each situation will present a unique set of circumstances to which creative faculty will have to respond. Funding or release time for team teaching can be difficult to obtain, requiring instructors to define responsibilities carefully so that no one becomes overloaded. In some institutions scheduling could pose problems. Administrators do not always recognize the value of such projects, creating the possibility that considerable work can go unrecognized as well as unrewarded. Ideally, deans, relevant chairpeople, and faculty should all be approached and should all take an interest in the success of joint ventures of this kind.

The risks of collaboration accrue largely to the instructors involved, although the reputation of the WAC program can be at stake when the collaboration is highly visible, usually in a small college setting. To avoid reinforcing the distinction often made between content and style, collaborators will need to take time to explain what they're doing to their colleagues. Good record keeping can provide material for public presentation of the experience as well as make it easier for this team or another team to revise the course.

When collaboration breaks down, generally one person must cede authority to the other or the effort falls apart. Should an impasse occur, you can often transform a collaborative relationship into a simpler consultation. The person with the least investment becomes the consultant, and planning can continue with the lines of authority redrawn. If the WAC program has established criteria for affiliation, the WAC administrator can determine whether or not the course maintains its identity as a WAC course.

ALTERNATIVE MODELS OF COLLABORATION

Team teaching allows us to explore new ground that cannot be approached any other way. What we learn about how discourse communities function enhances our ability to teach writing in any situation. Because of the amount of labor involved, however, team teaching arrangements rarely endure for long. When team teaching is not feasible, alternative models for collaboration can also produce valuable results.

Common alternatives include paired or adjunct courses, usually a writing or writing intensive class attached to an existing course, often one that meets a distributional or similar type of requirement (see Graham, this volume). UCLA's English 100W, a two-credit writing workshop paired with a course outside English, is one model of an adjunct course. UCLA also offers a four-credit version, English 110W. The University of Washington (also described by Graham), the University of California at Santa Barbara, the University of Southern California, and Illinois State University have other versions of collaborative courses.

Many WAC programs, including ours at the University of Pennsylvania, depend on collaboration among writing instructors and teaching assistants (TAs) in the disciplines who teach writing in their own departments. Although such arrangements tend to bypass faculty, the value of the collaboration is not significantly diminished. Programs that aim to influence TAs across the curriculum have the virtue of influencing the faculty of the future.

PROSPECTS FOR THE FUTURE

The department-based authority structure that characterizes most American colleges and universities today restricts many WAC activities to the margins of the curriculum. Formal collaboration and team teaching suffer from marginalization and have proven difficult to institutionalize. Yet much can be learned from experiments, and when viewed as a learning experience, collaborative ventures have much to offer WAC programs. Receptive faculty have a great deal to teach each other as well as their students about the practicalities of discourse communities and their day-to-day operation, including often critical information about the specific institution sponsoring the collaboration. This information can help the WAC program chart its course and maximize its effectiveness in its particular situation. Perhaps most important, the bonds formed through collaboration enrich WAC and bring us closer to our goal of creating a community of readers and writers that reaches across disciplines and helps break down the barriers that divide students and teachers from each other.

APPENDIX: COURSE DESCRIPTION FOR COMMUNICATIONS AND TECHNOLOGY PROBLEM SOLVING IN A HUMAN CONTEXT

This course is especially designed to help engineers become writers and public speakers. It is also designed to place the field of engineering in a human context, encouraging students to recognize that communication about any subject takes place between people. Consequently, effective communication requires much more than mastery of the subject or the mechanics of writing and speaking; it requires sensitivity to the needs of all people involved in the transaction, especially to the needs of the audience without whose active involvement no communication can take place.

Because this is an advanced course, we assume that students are familiar with grammar, punctuation, the rudiments of good style, and basic modes of organization. As a result, we will focus on larger issues of communication: writing for different purposes; controlling a variety of forms and styles; organizing complex material; expressing complicated ideas in simple terms; reaching different audiences; using analogy, metaphor, and other means to facilitate understanding; finding a satisfactory speaking voice; and establishing oneself as writer.

Because problem solving is a mode of thinking with which engineers feel comfortable, we have chosen that mode of representing the various activities associated with effective communication. We will approach both reading and writing activities from this perspective, focusing on defining problems and working out strategies to solve them. Because creative problem solving demands creative thinking, we will emphasize the critical role played by imagination as well as the foundation provided by logic and solid reasoning skills.

We chose the required readings for this course with these goals in mind. Through them we offer students models of the variety of writing about technical subjects that exists and stimulation to think about technology, and especially communication about technology, in a broad, human context. We also believe that reading and writing are related activities. To acquire effective communication skills, you must become a critical reader as well as a competent writer.

We have planned this course as a seminar and expect significant class participation. Part of the time we will adopt a workshop format, listening to speeches or working as a class or in teams on each other's writing. All students will receive regular feedback on their writing and speaking.

Brief Topic Outline

1. Defining the problem: What constitutes good writing?
   Problem-solving strategies in writing
   Writing as decision making
   Setting and reaching concrete goals
   Language and the art of communication
   Writer, reader, and text
   Writing and speaking as social acts
2. Exploring ideas: How can you expand your thinking?
   Thinking and writing
   Creative thinking and creative writing
   The role of ideas in writing

Brainstorming and other methods for expanding thinking

Methods for blocking and facilitating communication

3. Informing the public: How can you communicate technical information effectively to a nontechnical audience?

The right to know

Accuracy versus getting the general idea

Creating an informed reader

Analogy, metaphor, and other means of increasing understanding

4. Reporting to your peers: How do you communicate effectively with technical readers?

The language of scientific investigation

Objectivity and the voice of authority

Techniques for organizing information

The conventions of technical communication

5. Instructing consumers: How can you teach people what you know?

Identifying the audience

Asking the right questions

Creating knowledge and understanding

Demystifying technology

6. Proposing: How do you influence people to believe what you believe?

Influencing, arguing, and persuading

Getting your reader's attention

Creating a shared vision

7. Communicating in a human context: How can engineers become writers?

Overcoming specialization

Developing a personal voice

Risk-taking and effective communication

Technology and literature

Course Requirements

There will be four formal and two less-formal writing assignments for this class as well as two speaking assignments, one shorter (5 minutes) and one longer (15 minutes). The four formal papers will include a technical report, a set of instructions, a proposal, and an essay. Each of these will be addressed to a different audience and written for a different purpose. Your classmates will be your audience for your oral presentations. You are free to choose your subjects, but the first one must be to inform and the second to persuade. I will provide detailed information about each assignment when the time comes.

The procedural requirements for this course are very specific. Please read them through carefully and raise any questions you might have now.

1. Because this is a small class and work missed cannot be made up, attendance is mandatory.

2. All reading and writing assignments must be completed on time for students to benefit from discussion of them.

3. Drafts of the four major writing assignments and informal writing and speaking activities, although not graded, are required and must be done on time.

4. At least three conferences, spaced more or less evenly throughout the semester, are required. These may take place during reserved Writing Lab hours or during office hours.

5. Conscientious responses to the writing and speaking of classmates will help you develop your own skills as writers and speakers and are required. Ability to work effectively as part of a team will also be evaluated.

6. In lieu of an exam, we will ask you to turn in a folder of your work at the end of the semester, accompanied by a letter explaining how you have satisfied the requirements for the course and what you have learned.

Because the word processor has become an essential tool for writers, we expect that you will do most of your writing on a computer. The Writing Lab on the fourth floor of Bennett Hall is available to students in this class.

The books for this course are available at the Penn Book Center. They include:

Conceptual Blockbusting by James Adams
Problem-Solving Strategies for Writing by Linda Flower
Revising Prose by Richard Lanham

Soul of a New Machine by Tracy Kidder
Double Helix by James Watson
Zen and the Art of Motorcycle Maintenance by Robert Pirsig
Brooklyn Bridge: Fact and Symbol by Alan Trachtenberg

You should also pick up a bulk pack of readings at the copy center.

NOTE

1. I would like to acknowledge Jacob Abel, professor of mechanical engineering at the University of Pennsylvania, my collaborator on the engineering course, and Carol Schilling and Kay Rickard, the graduate assistants who researched and first taught the class. I would also like to acknowledge Andrea Hollingsworth, the professor of nursing with whom I team taught.

WORKS CITED

Bizzell, Patricia. "Cognition, Convention, and Certainty: What We Need to Know About Writing." *Pre/Text* 3 (1982): 213-43.

Faigley, Lester, and Kristine Hansen. "Learning to Write in the Social Sciences." *College Composition and Communication* 36 (1985): 140-49.

Fulwiler, Toby, and Art Young, eds. *Programs That Work: Models and Methods for Writing Across the Curriculum*. Portsmouth, NH: Boynton, 1990.

Herrington, Anne. "Classrooms as Forums for Reasoning and Writing." *College Composition and Communication* 36 (1985): 404-13.

Jolliffe, David A., and Brier, Ellen M. "Studying Writers' Knowledge in Academic Disciplines." *Writing in Academic Disciplines*. Ed. David Jolliffe. Norwood, NJ: Ablex, 1988. 35-87.

Kinneavy, James. "Writing Across the Curriculum." *Teaching Composition: 12 Bibliographical Essays*. Ed. Gary Tate. Fort Worth: Texas Christian P, 1987. 353-77.

McCarthy, Lucille P., and Barbara Walvoord. "Models for Collaborative Research in Writing Across the Curriculum." *Strengthening Programs for Writing Across the Curriculum*. Ed. Susan H. McLeod. San Francisco: Jossey-Bass, 1988. 77-89.

Pirsig, Robert M. *Zen and the Art of Motorcycle Maitenance: An Inquiry Into Values*. New York: Morrow, 1974.

Sontag, Susan. *Illness as Metaphor*. New York: Vintage Books, 1978.

Trachtenberg, Alan. *Brooklyn Bridge: Fact and Symbol*. Chicago: University of Chicago Press, 1979.

TEN

The Writing Center and Tutoring in WAC Programs

MURIEL HARRIS

Working with student writing is one of academia's most labor-intensive activities. All writers need—and benefit from— readers with whom they can interact as a paper takes shape, skilled coaches who can offer appropriate guidance as the writer moves through the various writing processes, and responders who can offer meaningful response to and evaluation of a final draft. In WAC programs as in composition classes, that evaluator is appropriately the instructor who reads the last draft of a student's paper in the context of the goals of the course and of the student's growth as a scholar. But those other types of interaction, the more collaborative efforts of readers and coaches, are also needed. Writing, as we have come to recognize, is neither a solitary activity nor solely the product of the writer. The elaboration of theories of the social nature of writing have helped those in the field of composition to acknowledge what writing center specialists have known since our earliest interaction with students in tutorials: Writers need knowledgeable, skilled collaborators. Some WAC instructors, however, go it alone; they are both the collaborators and evaluators, handling course content and all phases of assistance with student writing for the course. But such instructors are not only shortening their expected life span, they are also very likely to be short-changing their students. Making available tutorial assistance with writing is a far better option, which is why tutoring offered through a writing center is thus not only a widely practiced feature of WAC programs but also pedagogically and theoretically a sound approach. But this assumes two considerations, both of which need further examination: first, that there is a rationale for tutoring writing and, second, that there is a rationale for tutoring through a writing center.

RATIONALE

Advantages of Tutoring

In universities such as Oxford and Cambridge, tutors are so firmly entrenched in the academic system that rationales are rarely discussed, but in American institutions where the weight of historical precedent argues strongly for the model of learning via teacher-as-deliverer-of-knowledge (with all the concomitant passivity on the part of the student that this approach inherently mandates), there is a need to look at the implications of an alternate pedagogy such as tutoring. A major factor that differentiates tutoring from traditional instruction is that it involves collaborative learning, an assumption that student and tutor actively work together in order for the student to move forward and acquire new skills. A helpful analogy for this is that of tutor-as-coach, a common metaphor (Harris "Roles a Tutor Plays") because it readily calls to mind the role of the coach who stands at the sidelines (not in the center of the playing field), offering encouragement and advice based on experience and training, while the player expends the needed effort to succeed. Or, from a different perspective, Albert DeCiccio describes tutoring as operating on the principle of "shared authority" which offers a process of conversation and support that "empowers writers and tutors alike who constantly see the world anew . . . making use of the process of negotiation and compromise to reach insight and to achieve identification" (12).

Tutors, because they function in a nonevaluative, supportive environment, offer writers the opportunity to write, think, and talk with someone who through this collaborative talk and questioning helps the writer use language to develop ideas, to test possibilities, to re-see and rethink in the light of feedback from the tutor. McLeod, in "Defining Writing Across the Curriculum," describes this kind of talk as heuristic and clarifying. Other kinds of tutorial talk introduce students to the language and conventions of the academic discourse community for which they are writing. Peer tutors are especially helpful with this as they are particularly sensitive to the possible confusions and stumbling blocks their fellow students might encounter as they seek to enter what may be a bewildering new world. Tutorial conversations are also helpful in providing opportunities to try out and learn how to use the language appropriate for that community. Peer tutors, with a foot in each camp—as students themselves and as more experienced writers—become bridges to this new discourse community. Recognizing this, one peer tutor in our writing laboratory astutely (although perhaps a bit cynically) described this process as helping fellow students "learn how to toss around the power lingo of the field."

Equally important to students' developing independence as writers is that they can ask peer tutors more honest questions in the collaborative setting of a tutorial. Such questions are all too often the ones teachers wish students would ask in class but ones that they won't because of a mistaken fear of appearing inadequate. "This is probably a stupid question, but . . ." is often an opening gambit in a tutorial that initiates a very useful discussion because the student has voiced an honest concern or confusion. Moreover, writers working with tutors are free from the constraints of listening primarily for what the teacher wants (a major goal in any dialogue with a teacher about a paper) because the tutor's comments can be ignored, rejected, or built on. As a tutor I have learned that when a student puts aside what I've just offered with a comment like "Well, okay, I see why you're asking that, but what I think I want to emphasize here is . . .", the tutorial is doing exactly what it should be doing, helping the writer through dialogue to develop her own ideas, not what she thinks will please or pacify me. To accomplish all this, tutors need to be available through all phases of writing, from the earliest planning, through drafting, and into revising. The ability to individualize and to truly attend to each writer's needs, questions, and problems also means that tutors accomplish more when they meet with a student through various stages of writing than is possible when a writer brings in a last draft that is less open to change. (Most student writers clutching a last draft as they enter a writing center are more often interested in proofreading for sentence-level errors than they are in receiving feedback, comments, and suggestions. Students who come in with a paper already graded get little more than a postmortem.)

Advantages of a Writing Center

Tutors also function effectively when they are working in the supportive environment of a writing center. The ability of a tutor to be a peer and to establish the kind of relationship that permits honest dialogue and openness means that tutors are not teachers. Once they become, in Kenneth Bruffee's famous phrase, "little teachers" (463), they are no more than front-line graders wielding the first of the red pencils that students will encounter. Collaboration does not thrive in such an atmosphere. But if we recognize that a major strength of tutors is that they are not teachers, that they usually inhabit some middle world between the less experienced writer (or two untrained writers in a classroom peer response group) and the more experienced and knowledgeable teacher, we must also recognize that tutors too need support, assistance, and guidance. Working in the context of a writing center means that the tutor has easy access to the director, to a support group of other tutors, to materials and resources, and to meetings where tutors can ask for help in solving problems. But there are other and equally valid rationales for having a WAC tutoring program based in a writing center.

When a WAC program works with or through a writing center, there is a visible focus, a focal point, a place for writing on campus, a center for writing. Such a room will be stocked with resources, will be available for students during most working hours, will have a support staff to handle appointments and direct students to appropriate resources, and will have a director to run training programs for tutors and workshops for students and faculty. The message to students who come into a busy writing center, amid the noise, informality, coffee pot (and/or popcorn machine), and tables where people are talking vigorously is a particularly powerful one. Here is a place where writers write, where they talk, where there is institutional commitment to writing, where it is apparent that writing is a very real activity for students all over campus. This environment says that collaboration is a normal part of writing and that writers really do write for readers. Writers in the midst of other writers also learn that they are not the only ones who are apprehensive or overwhelmed by a writing task. Because we talk about discourse communities, communities of writers, and reader/writer negotiation of text, we should recognize that bringing a student into a roomful of writers and readers at work is a vivid demonstration of the social nature of writing.

We should also recognize, on a more practical plane, that students' lives are as busy and complicated as ours and that having a writing center, a place open and available at all convenient hours, means that they will use it more appropriately—when they really need help. Because of this, most writing centers have extensive drop-in or walk-in hours, times when students come in for unplanned for tutorials because that's when the need arises or when they are ready to work on their writing. My years of tutoring have proven to me that many of the most productive tutorials I have been in have been with students dropping in because they have been working on their paper in the library (or their room) and come to the writing center because they are actively thinking of how the paper will develop, what should be included, who the reader is, how the information should be organized, and all those other real concerns of writers. In a drop-in tutorial students rarely need a few minutes to shuffle through their notes to see what they wanted to talk about (or what it was that they are supposed to be writing about). Planned appointments are, of course, a more organized way to work, but they also have less immediacy. They tend to occur not when the writer is in the midst of thinking and writing. For this reason, some writing centers are situated in libraries or residence halls, to take advantage of the ability to be at the right place at the right time.

Writing centers also contribute to the growth and success of a WAC program, because they can often open new lines of communication to faculty who become interested in WAC after their students have used the center. Because most writing centers are open to the whole student population on campus, students find their way there even when faculty have not encouraged them to seek out tutorial assistance. A faculty member whose student suddenly shows noticeable improvement, who receives and attends to the tutorial report sent from the center, or who hears from the student about a successful trip there may call to thank the director or to inquire about the center's services. An enterprising director who fields such phone calls and follows them up with a visit to the faculty member's office often finds instructors interested in adding more writing to their courses. Sometimes even a negative faculty response can be turned into a positive one. For example, the end result of a recent call to our writing lab by a faculty member disgruntled with a tutor's note to him (after a student in one of his political science courses had come to the lab) was that the faculty member got far more information than he intended to solicit when he asked somewhat irately, "So what do you people do over there?" (His concern was that the tutor might have written the paper for the student.) Having heard what tutoring is all about, he is at present negotiating with his department head to fund a political science tutor in our lab to work with courses in his department.

THE STRUCTURE AND SERVICES OF A WRITING CENTER IN A WAC PROGRAM

Some Basics: Facilities, Services, Staff, and Training

Although writing centers all too often manage to cope with whatever physical facilities are assigned to them, a center with intentions of operating successfully should have a large, conveniently located room that is comfortably furnished and looks inviting. Round tables are needed so that tutors and students can talk side by side, not in the adversarial relationship created by desks. It is important to have couches, plants, a coffee pot, and whatever else announces to students that they have come to a friendly place where they can drop the passive, submissive student role and become active members of helpful discussions. Students forced to enter a cold, rigidly structured or formal classroom setting will not easily enter into the collaborative work that is essential for successful tutorials. The room should also be set up with areas for small group workshops, have cabinets full of helpful instructional handouts, bookshelves filled with appropriate reference books, and a reception desk with clerical help to greet students, direct them to appropriate tutors, answer that constantly ringing phone, and keep records. If possible, the room should also have computers for student use and some self-instruction materials—if and only if students want them. A center whose rationale is that students need and benefit from individualized help should have available a variety of instructional materials, in a variety of instructional modes so that all students can choose according to their preferred modes of learning. Do they want to talk to a tutor? Listen to a tape on commas? Take home a handout with some visually appropriate diagrams? Try an interactive computer program? Sit quietly by themselves at a table near some needed references and resources?

When students meet up with tutors, they should be working with other students who have been trained to talk in useful ways, to question, to listen, to offer feedback, and to explain, when needed. The tutor should know how to assess the situation, gather the needed information, start the tutorial off on a friendly, encouraging note, and have a variety of tutorial strategies to use. The training provided can be by means of credit-bearing courses (often highly prized résumé items and valued by education departments that recognize the value to prospective teachers in being involved in this different kind of experiential learning), presemester workshops, and/or in-service weekly meetings. Resources for such training include a number of tutor-training manuals (see B. Clark; I. Clark; Harris, *Teaching;* Meyer and Smith.)

The staff to be trained can be undergraduates who can be compensated by hourly wages or course credit, graduate students, professionals, volunteers, faculty, and retirees in the community. The director who oversees all this has a variety of responsibilities,because that person must set the goals and operating philosophy, hire and train staff, purchase or develop instructional materials, publicize the facility, handle the budget, act as liaison with faculty, meet with administrators and write reports—especially those crucial end-of-the-semester reports and evaluations of the center's work—develop new services, plan for future growth and development, and cope with the daily crisis management that seems to define the nature of writing centers.

WAC Coordination

The major concern of a writing center director who either directs the WAC program, assists the WAC director, or is on a campus where there is a WAC program is that of coordinating the work of the writing center with the faculty involved (see Hilgers and Marsella ch. 7). At Lehigh University, Edward Lotto's approach to integration of the writing center and the writing-intensive courses was to interview instructors and collect information about various faculty members' perceptions of what constitutes good writing in their discipline and what the problems are when students write papers for their courses. Lotto's goal was to build a picture of the differences in various disciplinary contexts for writing that would help tutors work appropriately with students writing for different disciplines. Another way to integrate the writing center with the faculty is to hold orientation meetings at the beginning of the semester. At this meeting, the director can review the goals of the center and its policies, suggest ways to encourage students to come to the center, and listen to the faculty share ideas about how they see the center meshing with their course work. At the end of the semester another meeting can be a time for discussing problems and sharing accomplishments.

Integration can also be achieved by means of training tutors in the center and then attaching them to specific courses. In some WAC programs, tutors attend classes and either tutor in the center or spend some of their tutoring hours working in an area near the faculty member's office. Other tutors meet with the faculty member and learn what the expectations are, how the assignments are structured, and what is expected of them. At Troy State University, the writing center serves as the base for their WAC program, with the WAC coordinator working in the center and supervised by the center's director. Troy State's center is responsible for preparing materials that are used in workshops held in the center. Workshop topics requested by the faculty include writing concerns such as how to handle various documentation styles or how to write book reviews, critiques, position papers, progress reports, abstracts, and so on (Lee). The emphasis of the WAC program at Troy State is writing to learn, an approach chosen after a survey conducted by the writing center director (World). A somewhat different—and unique model—is the writing center at the University of Maryland where students working on papers for the university's upper-level writing requirement can find retired professionals who volunteer as tutors in the center. Thus a student working on a management paper may meet with a retired businessman; a student doing a paper for a government class is likely to work with a retired lawyer.

At Montana State University, Carol Peterson Haviland describes the writing center's WAC projects as being of three types: those primarily involving faculty, those primarily involving students, and those involving faculty and students. The faculty-centered projects include assistance with designing writing assignments and presenting them to classes as well as help with evaluating writing, the projects for students are workshops held in the center, and the faculty/student projects focus on collaborative instruction in classrooms and one-to-one collaboration in the writing center. Haviland reports that their College of Nursing found the integration and collaboration with the writing center so effective that a center staff member has been asked to participate at the college's faculty meetings. Other signs of the success of this model are that the number of participating faculty grew in three years from fewer than a dozen to more than 100, that broad faculty support has brought permanent funding for the WAC program, and that students are using the writing center more productively, coming in earlier with rough drafts rather than at the last minute for proofreading help. At Lawrence University, Geoff Gajewski reports that their system of having tutors who are assigned to courses meet initially with instructors before even meeting with each student—to set the goals for the tutoring and to learn the instructor's expectations—results in a partnership between the faculty and writing center that stresses joint responsibility for the student's growth.

Despite the variety of ways in which writing centers are structured to work with the particular features of the WAC program on their campus, it is apparent that an increasing part of writing center directors' responsibilities is their work with faculty across campus. A survey, conducted by Joan Mullin, of more than 100 writing center directors indicates that greater than 50% of the directors reported that they act as consultants to various classes across campus or to the faculty. Many directors reported on their expanding roles in WAC programs, being asked to hold faculty workshops, to educate teaching assistants in composition theory and conferencing techniques, to handle requests for tutors in classrooms, to serve as consultants to departments developing writing intensive courses, to sit in on classes to see how writing can be incorporated into the course, to serve as a campus resource for writing in various disciplines, and to collect from the faculty articles on discipline-specific writing. Mullin, who serves as the writing center and WAC director at the University of Toledo, also coordinates a bimonthly writing workshop of faculty members who read their works in progress to each other and "discuss writing in general, exchange journals which welcome interdisciplinary writing, and serve as resources for grants, and have devoted a meeting to the writing of successful (and unsuccessful) grants" (12). At Boise State University, the director of the writing center, Rick Leahy, issues a widely read campus newsletter, *Word Works*, to assist faculty adding writing assignments and to keep them abreast of composition pedagogy. Subjects discussed in *Word Works* include designing assignments; writing the research paper; writing the long research report; writing the summary, the synthesis, and the critical analysis; using discussion and peer-response groups; creating short write-to-learn assignments; using journals; responding to student writing; and responding to the writing of students learning English as a second language. A reader survey of the faculty brought responses from all over the campus, including comments from faculty members who noted that they used ideas from the newsletter in their teaching and that they had applied ideas to their own writing.

Offering workshops for faculty and students is a frequent activity in many writing centers. For faculty interested in learning what they can expect their students to gain from tutorial instruction, workshops focus on topics such as what goes on in a tutorial, what faculty should expect from tutorial help, and what goes on in tutorials (with mock tutorials as examples). Other workshops for faculty deal with structuring assignments by reviewing effective and ineffective assignments or by having tutors discuss student difficulties with papers on various topics. Workshops in classes can offer brief reviews on topics that instructors request. For example, "to build bridges with departments across campus"

(Fitzgerald 13) the director of the University of Missouri-St. Louis Writing Lab talked with instructors so that she could offer lecture demonstrations in classes to explain the instructors' writing assignments, to review research skills, to offer information on format and documentation, and to discuss writing processes. An alternative to such in-class workshops are the noncredit short courses held in the Writing Lab at the University of Wisconsin-Madison (Feirn).

Writing centers can provide a variety of other services to assist campus writing activities. For example, offering computers in the center and providing students with instruction in word processing ensures that students in all courses have access to this effective technology. Most centers offer a variety of handouts for students, some tailored to specific courses and others geared to general writing needs such as methods for handling sources, distinctions between paraphrasing and plagiarizing, strategies for proofreading (a particularly popular handout in our lab), punctuation rules, general guidelines for good writing (such as handouts from the Writing Center at Harvard, distributed by Linda Simon at the 1988 Conference on College Composition and Communication), and so on. Students also use our lab to meet for peer editing sessions assigned by teachers (and are joined by peer tutors when teachers request this), to read journal entries to each other, and to locate material or do research for their papers. For example, sociology students come to our Writing Lab to observe students from other cultures as they interact with tutors; educational psychology students come in to study the use of different learning styles by students in the lab; business and organizational communication students observe the flow of communication in our large, busy facility; technical writing students write manuals for our computer users; and graduate students in our doctoral program in rhetoric and composition study tutorial instruction in writing. Similarly, the new writing center at the University of Illinois plans to have a research component on writing.

GETTING STARTED

When a writing center is first established, the most important work of the new director is to define the goals of the center and to see that the center is appropriately integrated into the writing program at that particular institution. Writing centers exist in many forms and shapes, but the most successful ones are not merely clones of other centers the prospective director has seen, read about, or heard a description of at a conference. Writing centers must take their shape in ways that meet the needs of the particular students and faculty on that campus and must be flexible enough to continue to grow as the writing program grows and develops. Typically, writing centers expand to meet perceived needs, adjust to changing conditions, and develop in close coordination with the director's growing awareness of what a writing center can really offer a particular program. But this is not to say that there is not a wealth of general information and resources about writing centers that introduces newcomers to the more theoretical perspectives as well as to the nuts-and-bolts information that is needed when starting up a tutoring center (these resources include Harris, *Tutoring;* Harris, *Writing Centers;* National Writing Centers Association; *Writing Center Journal; Writing Lab Newsletter).* The National Writing Centers Association meets twice a year, at the National Council of Teachers of English and at the Conference on College Composition and Communication.[1] Various regional groups that hold yearly conferences are coordinated through the national organization and are announced regularly in monthly issues of the *Writing Lab Newsletter.* The two publications the *Writing Center Journal* and the *Writing Lab Newsletter* differ in that the *Writing Center Journal* is published 2 times a year and contains journal-length articles focusing on theory and research and the *Writing Lab Newsletter* is published 10 times a year and contains brief articles focusing on practical aspects of writing center administration and pedagogy.

Major practical considerations for any new center include the following: (1) choosing the home base for the center (e.g., whether it will be a university service administered through a dean's office or a student services office or whether it will be an English department facility), (2) preparing the physical facility, (3) deciding on the services to be offered, (4) setting up the budget for operating expenses, (5) developing the administrative structure (e.g., record keeping, scheduling, and so on), (6) establishing a tutor-training program, and (7) constructing an evaluation system. The published resources listed above deal with these issues as do conference presentations on writing centers at the yearly meetings of the Conference on College Composition and Communication (in March), the National Council of Teachers of English (in November), and the numerous regional writing center association conferences held throughout the year. The National Writing Centers Association provides contact information for these regional associations, and both the *Writing Center Journal* and the *Writing Lab Newsletter* regularly announce meetings.

When new writing centers are being established to coordinate with WAC programs or when existing centers expand to work more closely with writing across campus, there are also some special considerations tied to this role. In particular, there are three concerns that have to do with working with students in content courses: (1) tutors should be selected and trained in ways consistent with the needs of working with discipline-specific writing, (2) appropriate resources should be added to the center, and (3) lines of communication should be established with instructors in content courses and with the WAC director—if that person is not already a part of the writing center.

When tutors are to be selected and trained for working with writing in content courses, one of the first questions directors must confront and answer for themselves is the degree to which the tutor should be familiar with the content matter. Should directors seek out and train potential tutors from the disciplines intending to refer students, or should the director rely on traditional pools for tutors in writing centers such as English majors? Unfortunately, there is no quick answer to this, just as there is no guaranteed selection process when interviewing applicants for tutoring positions. As Susan Hubbuch, the director of the writing center at Lewis and Clark College, reminds us, tutors "cannot afford to be parochial, entering a session with a student with an inflexible, monolithic concept of 'good' writing" (25), a concept that might be forged from knowing only the writing conventions of papers for English courses and thinking that "good" writing is whatever she has produced and been rewarded for in these classes. When Hubbuch examines the merits of the knowledgeable tutor (one who to some extent knows the content of the student's field), she notes that such tutors know the questions to ask and they know the necessary technical information about the writing conventions of that field. But they are prone to giving answers or taking an authoritative stance that can drive the student back to a passive role. Training for such tutors must include strong reminders of the ease with which they can slip into this role. An advocate of selecting tutors from other disciplines, Leone Scanlon, offers an overview of the content of a training course for such students in "Recruiting and Training Tutors for Cross-Disciplinary Writing Programs."

On the other hand, tutors who are ignorant of the subject matter may miss the important conventions that should be present. But they have the advantage of trying to understand the writer's argument from what they read in the paper, and as they do, they are forced to focus on the logic of the student's ideas. As Hubbuch notes, this in turn forces the student to explain what needs to be explained. It also, I have found, forces the writer to examine her reader's knowledge more closely. "Will your reader know the background you just explained to me?" I ask, thereby requiring the writer to reexamine who the intended reader really is or what the purpose of the piece of discourse is. Questions a tutor unfamiliar with the content must ask may lead back to the purpose of such a paper and can sometimes help a writer re-see the whole project. For example, when a student writing a summer internship report for a political science professor came to our writing lab with only a vague two-page draft (and some angry comments by the professor demanding that she expend more effort), I had great difficulty understanding the content, which focused on intricacies of how members of the British House of Commons prepare for daily sessions of the House. Seeing my struggle with both the facts and the terminology, the student poured out all sorts of useful information. Why, I asked, wasn't any of that wealth of information she had gained through her summer work in the paper? Her explanation, given in the patient tone of a parent explaining the obvious to a child, was that the professor knew all that. Once we redefined the purpose of the paper—to demonstrate to the professor what she had learned from her internship, not to offer the professor new insights—she was able to produce a highly informative, lengthy report. My ignorance had been the catalyst for a conversation in which she could see by her explanations to me how much she had learned.

The uneasiness I feel when enmeshed in details and jargon of a field I know little about is a common one among nonspecialist tutors, and it needs to dealt with in training sessions. For directors who choose nonspecialists in the various disciplines, the training course should include some attention to discipline-specific concerns as well as the general principles of writing that pervade all effective writing. Inviting faculty to tutor-training meetings to talk about their discourse communities is particularly useful and helps to dispel tutors' fears of reading papers in fields where they are out of their own area of expertise. One solution for this is to offer tutors some basic introduction to the content of a field. For example, James Murphy, in "Tutors and Fruitflies," notes that at Clarion University when a genetics professor asked for writing center help with his students' papers, he offered a one-hour lecture on basic genetics to the tutors.

He then invited teams of tutors to come to his classes and take over sessions devoted to working on the papers for the course. The students, initially hostile to unknowledgeable tutors, were surprised to find out that they learned more about genetics and writing than they had anticipated from the small group sessions with their peers and the tutors, and the tutors were equally surprised to learn that their lack of knowledge about genetics was not crucial to their effectiveness as tutors.

Identifying the pool from which to draw tutors is another factor that directors must consider. Potential tutors can be drawn from the ranks of upper-class students who have successfully taken writing intensive courses or who are recommended by faculty or who respond to general invitations issued to the student body. Some writing centers with low budgets make use of work/study students, offer course credit in lieu of salary, or draw tutors from service organizations on campus that have volunteers willing to donate time. Other writing centers seek tutors from among professionals in the community, recruit graduate students from other departments (Kristen Benson describes such a program at the University of Tennessee-Knoxville), or in the case of the writing center at the University of Maryland, rely partly on retired faculty and professionals from the community. In other cases, faculty staff writing centers at institutions where tutoring is recognized as part of faculty's teaching commitment or where faculty are given points toward promotion and tenure.

Letters for their files from the writing center director, as performance reviews, as letters of evaluation, or as letters of appreciation, are helpful.

One option for including faculty from different disciplines is to arrange for them to be available at specific hours and list in the center's brochure or announcement the hours when help is available, for example, with social sciences or fine arts. Students can work with these faculty members on the more discipline-specific concerns and with peer tutors for other aspects of planning, developing, and revising so that by mixing experience with both faculty and peer tutors, students can reap the advantages of working with both. This mix can be beneficial because faculty are, of course, not peers and cannot provide the setting for the kind of dialogue that peers engage in, but there are distinct advantages to having faculty in the center. The experience permits them to get a close look at the WAC program and at the advantages of tutoring. Such faculty may go on to become enthusiastic supporters of the writing center and the WAC program as well as far more knowledgeable classroom teachers when they structure their own assignments and respond to their own students' papers. For a more thorough discussion of the advantages to teachers of having been tutors, see Kate Gadbow's "Teachers as Writing Center Tutors: Release From the Red Pen."

Faculty who work as tutors in writing centers can also be active contributors to the center's resources. In a writing center with a commitment to working with writing in various disciplines, there have to be resources in addition to the usual instructional handouts on various aspects of writing and reference books. The center should establish collections of papers in various fields so that students can see models for the kinds of papers they will be writing and can see the variety of formatting concerns that exist. Articles and books on writing in various disciplines belong on the resource shelves as well as a number of reference books for different disciplines. In "The Writing Center: A Center for All Disciplines," Mary Pam Besser, the director of the writing center at Jefferson Community College in Tennessee, lists the following among the resources available to students in their writing center (pp. 184-85):

1. Handouts on writing in the humanities, the social sciences, the natural sciences, and the health sciences
2. Dictionaries (unabridged, etymology, foreign language [Latin, French, German, and Spanish], literary terms, social science terms, medical terminology)
3. Style manuals
   a. Modern Language Association (MLA)
   b. American Psychological Association (APA)
   c. *The Chicago Manual of Style*
   d. Council of Biology Editors (CBE)
   e. American Chemical Society
   f. American Mathematical Society
   g. *Style Manual for Guidance in the Preparation of Journals Published by the American Institute of Physics* (for Health Sciences)
4. Sample assignments and papers from various disciplines

PITFALLS TO AVOID

While writing centers can and do work effectively with writing in the disciplines, there are some potential problems that directors can stave off by some preventative maintenance work. Perhaps the most commonly perceived problem is one that all composition faculty recognize, that instructors in other fields don't quite know what we do when we teach writing. If faculty in other disciplines are prone to seeing writing instruction as merely the teaching of editing skills ("get them to spell correctly"), then writing centers have even more difficulty in helping faculty in other areas understand what the one-on-one, nonevaluative, collaborative, interactive, individualized nature of tutoring is. Well-meaning but unthinking faculty are prone to sending their students to the writing center with papers that have sentence-level errors to have the writer and/or the paper "fixed." Unfortunately, this is the same misperception shared by faculty in English departments, and writing center directors must patiently work toward educating faculty to recognize that writing centers are neither merely remedial facilities nor Band-Aid clinics for grammar errors. In 1985, Stephen North's article "The Idea of a Writing Center" articulated this concern, which remained just as real in 1988, when Diana George found that faculty with whom she talked didn't know what writing centers do, what they offer, or how they work with students. George also found faculty suspicious that tutors write the papers for students. Rick Leahy's solution to informing faculty and dispelling their misconceptions about writing centers was to devote one issue of his center's campus newsletter, *Word Works*, to this. (Leahy's article "Seven Myth-Understandings About the Writing Center" is reprinted in the *Writing Lab Newsletter*.)

Clearly, what is needed is extensive education: workshops with faculty in which the role of the writing center is explained or demonstrated and campus newsletters which continue the education process. Personal visits, contacts, discussions, and attendance at faculty meetings all help provide opportunities for the ongoing dialogue that can help faculty to know how and why they want their students to get tutorial help with papers. Having tutors come to classes, asking faculty to nominate prospective tutors, writing a user's manual for the center (see, for example, Harris's "A User's Guide"), and sending reports of tutorials are other means of keeping channels of communication open so that faculty will see that writing centers are used by all students for dialogues about writing not just by poor writers and that writing center visits are not punishments to be inflicted on students who have not performed as expected.

Just as students should not "be sent" to the writing center, faculty should not be mandated to participate in the center's workshops or tutoring programs for various courses. When faculty agree to participate because they have an interest in writing, they become, as Carol Peterson Haviland notes, "willing, interested collaborators." In turn, says Haviland, writing center directors should not dominate, not appear "as experts wafting in to transform someone else's teaching" (29). It is equally important, as Haviland notes, not to commit the mistake she did of being the person to introduce the writing assignment in the instructor's classroom. When she did, students grumbled about "having to do English in a nursing class." Instead, she encouraged the content instructor to present the writing tasks while she, as a representative of the writing center, was introduced as a resource. The transformation in student attitudes was, not unsurprisingly, "remarkable." "The English instructor became an ally, not a pest" (30).

The price of success, though, can be exhaustion. Successful writing centers that expand to meet all the various writing needs on campus, that serve large and thriving WAC programs, can send the center—and the director—into permanent overload. Writing center directors who step initially into budding programs to encourage writing in various courses can find themselves moving into a full-time WAC coordinating position, in addition to directing their centers. They need to remind themselves that no one but them knows that they are filling two (or more) full-time jobs. They and their administrators need to recognize that all the contact activity, workshop development, and attendance at various meetings represents a major expenditure of time. Assistance will be needed as their job description expands.

Equally important, administrators must recognize that when the writing center is overflowing, is covered wall-to-wall with students waiting for a tutor, more tutors will be needed. But the director needs to monitor this growth to see that quality does not fall by the wayside because of the pressures of quantity. Because there cannot be endless expansion, directors need to seek alternative solutions. Small group workshops on topics of general importance provide some reduction in the overload situation. Other solutions are discussed in Ray Wallace's "The Writing Center's Role in the Writing Across the Curriculum Program: Theory and Practice." At the University of Tennessee-Knoxville, where the WAC program is coordinated through the writing center. Wallace had to find solutions to counter the strain of an added program to the center's already overburdened mission. He found additional sources for tutors by turning to non-English majors, held two-day workshops with faculty in different disciplines to come to some general sense of what the instructors were all looking for in student writing (a time-saving solution as well as an effective way to coordinate faculty expectations), and developed a series of tutor-training sessions in which faculty came to discuss their assignments, course materials, and goals.

When there is a turnover in the instructors involved with WAC programs, writing center directors will have a pressing and continual need to educate new faculty members about the real nature of tutorial instruction and about the work of a writing center. Tutors will need help in working with new types of writing and must be kept up to date about writing assignments and requirements in various courses. Attuned to the relative stability of working with writers in composition courses where there is a standardized syllabus or where similar assignments are given, tutors will find themselves often treading into unknown waters. Directors need to keep a variety of people informed about each other's work. Although the pitfalls mentioned here are very real, they also indicate some of the benefits of having a tutorial center. Despite the heavy influx of students, the rapid growth, the changing nature of the writing assignments in different courses, and the often noisy, informal (and at times, downright messy) nature of a writing center, it is the support system on campus for collaboration in writing. Students come here to talk, to write, and to learn about writing. The comments they send back on evaluations are appreciative and heartfelt. They have learned about writing. They have come to a place that is a visible, tangible center for writing, the hub for writing across the campus.

NOTE

1. National Writing Centers Association's executive secretary is Nancy Grimm; the address is Department of Humanities, Michigan Technological University, Houghton, Michigan 49931.

WORKS CITED

Benson, Kirsten. "Who Will Staff the Writing Center." *Writing Lab Newsletter* 14.2 (1989): 13-16.

Besser, Mary Pam. "The Writing Center: A Center for All Disciplines." *Voices of Empowerment: Proceedings of the Eleventh Annual East Central Writing Centers Association Conference*. Ed. Lea Masiello. Indiana, PA: Halldin, 1990. 182-86.

Bruffee, Kenneth. "The Brooklyn Plan: Attaining Intellectual Growth Through Peer-Group Tutoring." *Liberal Education* 64 (1978): 447-68.

Clark, Beverly Lyon. *Talking About Writing: A Guide for Tutor and Teacher Conference*. Ann Arbor: U of Michigan P, 1985.

Clark, Irene. *Writing in the Center: Teaching in a Writing Center Setting*. Dubuque, IA: Kendall, 1985.

DeCiccio, Albert. "Literacy and Authority as Threats to Peer Tutoring." *Writing Lab Newsletter* 13.10 (1989): 1112.

Feirn, Mary. "Writing in the Health Sciences: A Short Course for Graduate Nursing Students." *Writing Lab Newsletter* 13.5 (1989): 5-8.

Fitzgerald, Sallyanne. "Successes and Failures: Facilitating Cooperation Across the Curriculum." *Writing Lab Newsletter* 13.1 (1988): 13-15.

Gadbow, Kate. "Teachers as Writing Center Tutors: Release From the Red Pen." *Writing Lab Newsletter* 14.2 (1989): 13-16.

Gajewski, Geoff. "The Tutor/Faculty Partnership: It's Required." *Writing Lab Newsletter* 15.10 (1991): 13-16.

George, Diana. "Talking to the Boss: A Preface." *Writing Center Journal* 9.1 (1988): 37-44.

Harris, Muriel. "The Roles a Tutor Plays: Effective Tutoring Techniques." *English Journal* 69 (1980): 62-65.

———. *Teaching One-to-One: The Writing Conference.* Urbana, IL: NCTE, 1986.

———. *Tutoring Writing: A Sourcebook for Writing Centers.* Glenview, IL: Scott, 1982.

———. "A User's Guide to Writing Centers." *Composition Chronicle* 1.9 (1989): 4-7.

———. *Writing Centers.* SLATE Starter Sheet. Urbana, IL: NCTE, 1988.

Haviland, Carol Peterson. "Writing Centers and Writing-Across-the-Curriculum: An Important Connection." *Writing Center Journal* 5.2/6.1 (1985): 25-30.

Hilgers, Thomas, and Joy Marsella. *Making Your Writing Program Work: A Guide to Good Practices.* Newbury Park, CA: Sage, 1992.

Hubbuch, Susan. "A Tutor Needs to Know the Subject Matter to Help a Student With a Paper: ___Agree ___Disagree ___Not Sure." *Writing Center Journal* 8.2 (1988): 23-30.

Leahy, Rick. "Seven Myth-Understandings About the Writing Center." *Writing Lab Newsletter* 14.1 (1989): 7-8.

Lee, Eleanor. "The Writing Center at Troy State University: A Multi-Service Learning Center." *Writing Lab Newsletter* 13.2 (1988): 1-4.

Lotto, Edward. "The Texts and Contexts of Writing," *Writing Center Journal* 9.1 (1988): 13-20.

McLeod, Susan. "Defining Writing Across the Curriculum." *WPA: Writing Program Administration* 11.1-2 (Fall 1987): 19-24.

Meyer, Emily, and Louise Z. Smith. *The Practical Tutor.* New York, Oxford U P, 1987.

Murphy, James. "Tutors and Fruitflies." *Writing Lab Newsletter* 15.9 (1991): 5-6.

Mullin, Joan. "Empowering Ourselves: New Directions for the Nineties." *Writing Lab Newsletter* 14.10 (1990): 11-13.

North, Stephen. "The Idea of a Writing Center." *College English* 46 (1985): 433-46.

Scanlon, Leone. "Recruiting and Training Tutors for Cross-Disciplinary Writing Programs." *Writing Center Journal* 6.2 (1986): 37-42.

Simon, Linda. "The Writing Center and Students Across the Curriculum." Conference on College Composition and Communication. St. Louis, Missouri. 19 Mar. 1988.

Wallace, Ray. "The Writing Center's Role in the Writing Across the Curriculum Program: Theory and Practice." *Writing Center Journal* 8.2 (1988): 43-48.

Writing Center Journal. Ed. Diana George and Nancy Grimm. Department of Humanities, Michigan Technological U, Houghton, MI 49931.

Writing Lab Newsletter. Ed. Muriel Harris. Dept. of English, Purdue U, West Lafayette, IN 47907.

Word, Joan. "TSU Surveys Campus Writing/Learning Practices." *Writing Lab Newsletter* 14.6 (1990): 14-16.

ELEVEN

Changing Students' Attitudes

Writing Fellows Programs

TORI HARING-SMITH

When I arrived at Brown University in the fall of 1980, the dean of the college (Harriet Sheridan) told me that my real task was to "do something about the problem of writing throughout the university." At the first faculty meeting, I listened as my colleagues offered unsolicited criticism of their students' writing, citing defects that ranged from poor spelling to inadequate research skills and weak critical thinking. How was I to address these concerns? How could I, as an untenured junior faculty member, ask senior colleagues to participate in a faculty development program—a foreign concept at most research institutions?

In my first year, I was able to accomplish two rudimentary but essential goals: I started a drop-in writing center housed in the library, and I saw that a column was added to the final grade sheets for all courses so that faculty could indicate those students whose writing they found inadequate. At the end of the year, then, I had a basic support system and a means of identifying students who needed help. Only a few people had to cooperate on these reforms: the space allocation committee (the dean approached them) and the registrar, who controls the printing of the final grade sheets.

Now all that was needed was a means of providing courses in which writing was emphasized and discussed. The English department writing courses were already oversubscribed—we turned away two students for every one we placed. Besides, the department did not want to increase its composition offerings for fear of disrupting the departmental balance between composition and literature. In short, it was clear that we needed a writing across the curriculum program. It was also clear that faculty outside the English department did not feel it was their responsibility to teach writing.

ASSUMPTIONS AND OBJECTIVES

To address this situation, we needed a program that was based on the two fundamental principles of WAC: shared responsibility among the faculty for helping students learn to write and the association of writing with learning. Because the reward system at research institutions does not focus as much on teaching as it does on research, we also needed to find a way of rewarding faculty who participated in this program. Finally, we needed a program that would address student as well as faculty attitudes toward writing. As Swanson-Owens has pointed out, working with faculty is sometimes not sufficient. Faculty, especially participating faculty, may see writing as part of the general culture of the community, inseparable from thinking. But for students, a WAC program can mean just a shift in terminology; instead of writing being the isolated concern of certain English classes, it is now the isolated concern of certain writing-intensive (WI) courses. (Indeed, not long ago I heard a student complain that a teacher should not have commented on his writing because the relevant course was not a WI course.)

It was important, then, to develop a program that defined and enacted a new role for writing, from both faculty and student perspectives. The program needed to do more than just increase the amount of writing that students did. Research suggests that merely increasing the amount without also attending to the students' writing processes does nothing to better their writing (see Haynes). The program needed to focus instead on the processes of writing and revising, working to counteract the popular student myth that good writers never revise.

The program should stress feedback and, most important, peer feedback for revision. As Sperling and Freedman have shown, students who receive feedback on drafts from their teachers often misunderstand that feedback, and because of the authority of the teacher sometimes feel obliged to revise in ways that do not always improve the paper. Peer feedback helps writers retain authority over their own texts. Furthermore, students needed to be able to discuss and revise their work before it was graded, so that revision was a natural part of writing, not a response to failure. The Writing Fellows Program that evolved at Brown, then, had eight major objectives:

- To demonstrate that all faculty and students share responsibility for student writing
- To explore ways in which writing and learning are connected
- To change both student and faculty attitudes toward writing
- To make writing an integral part of the curriculum, not a feature of isolated courses
- To encourage students to practice good writing habits, including revision
- To involve all students, not just the weak writers
- To reward faculty for their attention to student writing
- To provide students with feedback for revision before their writing is judged and graded

DESCRIPTION OF THE PROGRAM

To address these goals, Brown's cross-curricular writing program relies on a core of trained undergraduate peer tutors called writing fellows. (This title is regrettably gender-specific, but it does combine the notions of honor and of fellowship I wished to convey.) These tutors are selected from diverse disciplines and then trained (and paid) to serve as first readers for papers written in selected courses throughout the curriculum. The tutors comment on students' work as a reader would, noting areas where they as readers are confused (they do not have responsibility for factual or interpretive accuracy in the subject area of the course). They communicate with the writers they are tutoring through both written and face-to-face conferences, so that the writers have a chance to discuss and explain their intentions. Students need not take the advice of peer tutors (because, after all, the writer usually knows more about the subject than does the tutor); students retain authority over their texts. Ultimately, the faculty member receives two versions of the paper: the original with the writing fellow's comments and the revision based on those comments and on the conference. The faculty member reads and grades the final version, but the first version is available as evidence that the student has revised and that the tutor has neither misled the student nor served as ghost writer.

The Brown program might at first glance seem similar to peer tutoring programs based in writing centers (see Harris, this volume). There are, however, some differences. Writing fellows are not located in one central spot on campus, waiting for students to come to them; they are instead part of a course, coming to class to introduce themselves, collect and return papers, and arrange conference times. These conferences can take place all over the campus, interjecting discussions of writing into the dormitories, libraries, and snack bars as well as in classroom buildings. Furthermore, all students in a given course work with peer tutors, regardless of their abilities. No student needs to identify herself or be identified by a faculty member as needing help in order to participate in the program. Finally, the program differs from many housed in a writing center in that it assists individual faculty members with assignment design and models for them in a direct and immediate way methods of responding to student writing. (Because tutors work exclusively with one course they often learn how the mode of analysis for the discipline is evident in its discourse, and can help faculty see that connection.) Although this program serves only a selected number of courses each semester, these courses are selected from all levels throughout the curriculum, from freshman seminars to graduate courses; classes range in size from 6 to 350 students. Because more faculty want our services than we can help at any given time, we move our resources around; thus no one course becomes permanently identified as an enclave for concern about writing. There are currently 80 writing fellows working with about 2,400 students, out of a total undergraduate body of 5,000.

Faculty members wishing to have writing fellows in their courses apply to the program. In selecting among these applications, we are first concerned that the course satisfy our basic requirements. The course must include at least two significant writing assignments (significance is measured not only in terms of length—usually five to seven pages—but also in terms of role within the content of the course and weight in the final grade). In addition, faculty must agree that all students in the course will participate in the program, and that they, the faculty, will not change due dates for the papers without giving the writing fellows as well as the students fair warning. We try to maintain a balance among the disciplines to which we assign fellows; we put about 65% of the writing fellows in courses serving lower-division students, and the rest in upper-level courses.

If they are accepted, faculty are assigned one writing fellow for every 15 students in the class. Only with courses relying heavily on technical vocabulary or with foreign language courses must the writing fellows have particular expertise; the writing fellow in most courses acts as an educated lay reader, who can honestly report when she's confused by what a student is trying unsuccessfully to say. She does not need to "forget" what she knows about a subject to "feign" confusion. The lack of particular expertise also ensures that the writing fellows will not be confused with graders or teaching assistants. (For institutions that place writing fellows in courses in their major fields, it is important that faculty understand this distinction.)

We have found that large courses (more than 75) with no discussion sections do not work well; large courses in which small groups of students have a separate identity (as in a laboratory or discussion group)—so that writing fellows are working with the small groups—are fine. In the case of large courses, one or two writing fellows are designated head fellows and are paid a slightly higher stipend for their work. These head fellows run the program on a day-to-day basis within a specific course. Head fellows meet with the faculty before the semester begins to discuss the role of writing in the course and to look at the writing assignments the faculty plan to use. They ask faculty how students typically succeed and fail at their assignments and elicit information (like faculty preference for objective summary or for interpretation and argument) that will be helpful in their tutoring. These head fellows then collect student drafts and distribute the papers to other writing fellows assigned to the course. If the faculty member wishes to talk with all the writing fellows assigned to her class, she contacts the head fellow, who will assemble the group or pass on information. Head fellows also monitor the work of the writing fellows assigned to them, ensuring that all papers are returned on time and troubleshooting as necessary. From the faculty member's point of view, the program does not alter a course much at all. Although it immediately doubles the amount of writing students do (because each paper is written twice), it does not change the number of papers that faculty must read and grade. Furthermore, faculty can read the papers with greater ease because students are less likely to write disorganized, ill-conceived papers the night before the due date. This allows faculty to deal with substantive rather than surface features of student papers. The program does require, however, that faculty impose two due dates for each paper. Usually papers are due to the writing fellow from one to two weeks before the final drafts are due to the faculty member. During the first half of that period the writing fellows make written comments on the drafts; during the second half they meet with students in conference, and the students revise their work. This schedule sometimes requires that students draft their work before all the reading and lectures for a given unit of study have been completed. But as faculty soon discover, this procedure need not cause difficulties, because students' knowledge of the subject will grow as they work on their papers—as they write, they learn what they need to know, and as they learn more, they can rewrite. In a given semester, most writing fellows at Brown work with 15 students on two to three papers of five to seven pages each. Clearly, for a program like this to work, the writing fellows need to be selected and trained carefully. At Brown, writing fellows must be at least at the end of their second semester to apply for one of the 35 or so positions that are open each year. Applicants provide a list of courses they have taken, a list of extracurricular activities, a description of previous teaching/counseling experiences, and three samples of their writing (at least two of which must be critical or analytical). They are interviewed by two current writing fellows, after which both the interviewers and the applicants complete written evaluations. All these materials are reviewed by a committee of writing fellows and the two program administrators in order to select new writing fellows. When we make the selection, we are looking for certain characteristics. Successful writing fellows are students who can lead their peers without threatening them. They are articulate about their own writing processes and insightful in their analysis of others' writing. Their own writing shows the ability to write well in several different styles or rhetorical situations. They may not be the best writers in the institution, but they are dedicated to helping others write well, much as an editor who is not herself a superb writer can nevertheless give other writers helpful feedback.

Concurrent with their first semester in the program, all writing fellows at Brown take a full-credit course, Seminar in the Theory and Practice in Teaching Composition; the course is taught in three sections of no more than 13 students each. (During this time the writing fellows also carry a full tutorial load, a design which has proved difficult for some tutors. At Swarthmore College the Writing Associates in Training [WAITs] work with only three students during their first semester, assuming a full load in the spring. While this arrangement reduces stress during the training period, Thomas Blackburn, who runs Swarthmore's program, says that it delays the moment of "panic" when tutors must handle a full load of students.) The seminar addresses the role of the peer tutor, the issue of authority in education, the ways in which an academic audience and academic evaluation practices can affect developing writers, various methods of investigating and describing differences among disciplinary discourses, and the influence of gender and culture on the peer tutoring and writing processes. During the training course, writing fellows write and comment on each other's writing and practice commenting on student papers. Writing fellows are specifically trained to respond to papers as readers rather than to make judgmental comments. Instead of calling a paper "poorly organized" or "inadequately thought out," writing fellows are taught to pose questions or offer observations: "How is the discussion of X on page one related to the discussion of Y on page three?" "You say A on page three and B on page five. These seem like contradictions. I'm confused." (See the distinction Peter Elbow makes between criterion-based and reader-based comments, 237-63. For a full description of the course, see Haring-Smith.) When they have finished the first-semester training program, writing fellows work more autonomously, although they are still monitored by head fellows. They are also required to discuss each set of papers they comment on with the program director, associate director, or student assistant director. This provides the administrators of the program an opportunity to keep in touch with the writing fellows and to point out areas that they might ignore as they move away from the training period. The entire group of writing fellows meets once a semester for a retreat and refresher on responding to writing, as well as for a program evaluation.

In the first decade of the program's existence, word of it has spread to other institutions. By the most recent count there were more than 100 schools with some version of a writing fellows program. Even though it began at a research institution, the program works in many different settings: from two-year colleges like Monroe Community College in Michigan, to small liberal arts colleges like Swarthmore, Georgia Southern, and William Jewell, to large state institutions like Western Washington State and Rensselaer Polytechnic Institute. Neither the size of the institution nor the selectivity of its admission criteria seems to affect the success of the writing fellows program.

Each of the programs is, of course, different from the one at Brown, adapted to the situation at a particular institution. Some schools try using writing fellows as their first attempt at designing a WAC program, while others come to it after other approaches have failed. La Salle University's program emerged from an already established WAC program begun with faculty development seminars. The writing fellows program there was proposed by faculty from finance, biology, and economics who had been through WAC faculty workshops. Some institutions, like Williams College, do not attach the writing fellows to courses but affiliate the program with the writing center and coordinate the drop-in and the curricular support activities closely. Some institutions have associated the program with a particular group of students. At the University of Delaware it is the honors students (who live in the same dormitory and take most of their classes together) who serve as writing fellows; the funding comes entirely through the honors program. Knox College uses Ford Fellows as a group from which to draw writing fellows. Some institutions pay their writing fellows with university credit; most pay a fixed honorarium. The variations are as numerous as the schools involved. For anyone who would like to talk with those involved in these programs, the

National Conference on Peer Tutoring in Writing is a good place
to start. There are also regional meetings, for example the New
England Regional Conference on Peer Tutoring in Writing.[1]

HOW TO INITIATE AND MAINTAIN
A WRITING FELLOWS PROGRAM

Because these programs are not very costly, they can be started
easily and unobtrusively. (At Brown the program was first publicized as "a method for administering the writing requirement"
and was not discussed by the faculty until it had been in place for
one year.) All you need are a few willing students, someone to
train them and administer the program, and most important, the
cooperation of an administrator who will provide funding for the
program. The funding need not be magnificent; at Brown the
Writing Fellows Program was funded during the first three semesters through the same contingency fund that covered unexpected
heating costs. (As the program matures and proves its success, it
may be possible to find funding from other sources; businesses
and corporations that hire your graduates and who are interested
in employees who communicate well are good sources to approach. We recently received funding from Citibank, a company
that had hired a number of our former writing fellows.)

As with all writing across the curriculum programs, you should
work first with those key faculty who are open to innovations in
teaching, respectful of students, and trusted by colleagues. Those
faculty will be analytical and helpful as you develop the program.
Many of them will be campus leaders; other faculty will listen
when they talk about the program. After a year or so, you will be
ready for more trigger-happy skeptics to be involved, but at first
you will want to work among friends. As the program evolves, be
aware that it will grow and that you will need help. When the
program at Brown started up, I was the only administrator. But as
it grew from 20 writing fellows the first semester to 40 in the
second and 60 in the third, I found that I needed extra hands. You
will find that you can ask the writing fellows themselves to do
some of the work; the head fellows program was developed to
involve students in the day-to-day administration of the program.
The students need to own the program at several levels, and when

students are involved in administration as well as in tutoring, the program runs more energetically. The director must still maintain as much control as possible over the larger aspects of the program, however, because the politics of student-run programs can be difficult. Few people in higher education look to undergraduates as possible administrators; those who collaborate daily with students look to them first. You may find, however, that even after enlisting students for administrative tasks you need help on a more permanent basis. I continued to work with only student assistance until 1986, when we hired a very well qualified staff member as associate director. She alternates in teaching the training course and splits with me the work of overseeing the writing fellows. There is also an assistant director for our program, a position filled by an experienced writing fellow.

Most institutions that have initiated writing fellows programs find that both the writing fellows and the faculty with whom they work are positive—indeed, enthusiastic—about the program. Be aware, however, that the students affected by the program can have more mixed reactions. During the first few years when there are still students who remember a time before writing fellows, some may resent the additional work involved, especially if they are already confident about their writing and feel that good writers do not need to revise. After about three years, however, most students at Brown saw the program as a part of campus life, and came to think of revision and consultation with peers as a natural part of the writing process.

PITFALLS TO AVOID

Once the program is well established, other concerns emerge. The position of writing fellow can become coveted and highly competitive; while you want the program to carry a certain amount of prestige, it is important not to let the writing fellows become campus celebrities and lose the ability to relate to other students as peers. No institutionally recognized and authorized tutors can be true peers, of course, but there are a number of ways to combat the forces that would make them into a student version of instructional staff. Tutor training should make students aware of the possible status difficulties, and campus outreach programs can continually define and redefine the program for the campus community. Faculty advisors should be made aware of what the program entails and what the writing fellows do. On a residential campus, the director should be in touch with the student advisors who live in the dormitories, to ensure that these trusted student guides know the intentions behind the Writing Fellows Program.

Tutor burnout can also be a problem, especially after the first semester of training when tutors are no longer meeting together regularly. Retreats and other social events that bring the writing fellows back together are very important (Friday afternoon coffee breaks, for example, or brown-bag lunches). Writing fellows need to keep thinking about issues of peer collaboration and writing and have an opportunity to discuss newly published and relevant research. They might be encouraged to publish their own work locally, or in a publication like a writing center newsletter or journal. Most of all, they need a forum in which to talk to each other and to keep in touch with the director about their concerns.

The director also needs to keep in touch with the faculty involved in the program, because sometimes they want to place the Writing Fellow in the familiar role of teaching assistant (TA) or grader. As you involve faculty, you need to make sure that they understand the program and the distinct role of the writing fellow. Sometimes faculty need to be reminded of this role, since it is one unfamiliar to them. Faculty may also need assistance from the director with revising assignments to fit the program, setting the two due dates for each paper, or rethinking the ways they use writing in the classroom.

Finally, it is important not to let the program stagnate. Success can be paralyzing. The training course will need to change as the program matures; the administrative structure will need to change to accommodate growth. Sometimes the program will sprout new initiatives that must be fit in. For example, Brown (like several other institutions) has begun working on the integration of speaking with writing across the curriculum. We now offer additional training for some writing fellows so that they can provide feedback on students' oral assignments—formal debates, seminar paper presentations, leading class discussions. These "rhetoric fellows" are becoming increasingly popular and are encouraging faculty to reintroduce speaking into their curricula. The new focus has also revitalized those of us working with the writing fellows program (for more information on integrating speaking with writing across the curriculum programs, see *SAC*).

EVALUATION OF WRITING FELLOWS PROGRAMS

Like all WAC programs, writing fellows programs need to be carefully and consistently evaluated in order to remain vital. But program evaluation, as others have pointed out, is a tricky business (see Young and Fulwiler; Fulwiler; Witte and Faigley). Because writing fellows programs involve not just students but also tutors and faculty, evaluation measures should involve all three groups. At Brown, for example, every student who works with a writing fellow completes an evaluation form that asks for feedback on both the individual writing fellow's work and on the program as a whole. After we review the student evaluations, we send a report to each faculty member participating in the program and they may respond with a letter of evaluation, noting strengths and weaknesses of both individual writing fellows and of the program and responding to any concerns we may have raised. Writing fellows evaluate their training program and also evaluate their own work, noting what they concentrated on in their response to student writing, how well they worked with students and faculty, and evaluating the program's interaction with the course in which they worked. About every three years we undertake a more complete evaluation, interviewing students who work with writing fellows, the writing fellows themselves, and the faculty the program serves. Twice we have involved outside evaluators. Finally, we keep in touch with graduates of the program to see if the skills they learned as writing fellows affect them after they leave college. We have found that wherever they go (law school, medical school, the Peace Corps) our graduates frequently end up teaching in some capacity. We take this as a sign of the success of the program.

It is difficult, of course, to prove in an empirical sense that any writing program "works" (see White ch. 10). But if faculty, tutors, and students continue to tell you that it works, then something must be happening. Schools that institute these programs often find that faculty stop complaining about student writing. If a particular teacher takes a semester off from the program to let another class be involved, he or she will often invent ways of soliciting peer response because they had found the writing fellows procedure so valuable. Another measure of success is that the program often serves as a model for similar initiatives. At Brown, for example, we now have "science mentors" to help students through laboratories, "foreign language fellows" who are fluent in a second language and work with students in beginning language courses, and a program that allows faculty and students to collaborate to redesign or develop new courses for the curriculum. As one Writing Fellow put it, students have become not just peer tutors, but "disciples for curricular reform." Why might a would-be WAC director prefer this model over some of the others described in this book? Like all WAC programs, writing fellows programs aim at altering the role writing plays in the curriculum by redefining the writing process and linking it to learning. Writing fellows programs have the added virtue of providing writing instruction that is divorced from evaluation, and making that instruction available to all. Students learn a model for peer response and collaboration that extends beyond the usual vague commiseration, a model that is helpful not just in their writing, but in all their learning. It is also enormously rewarding for the tutors themselves; when students join the instructional ranks and take responsibility for advising one another, they learn as well. The program rewards faculty by helping with the paper load and letting them make better use of their time in commenting on papers. In short, these programs encourage faculty and students alike to feel like members of a community of writers. In this respect, a writing fellows program might be called not writing across the curriculum but rather writing throughout the community.

NOTE

1. For more information on peer tutoring conferences, contact Muriel Harris, Purdue University. See also Harris, this volume.

WORKS CITED

Elbow, Peter. *Writing With Power*. New York: Oxford U P, 1981.

Fulwiler, Toby. "Evaluating Writing Across the Curriculum Programs." *Strengthening Programs for Writing Across the Curriculum*. Ed. Susan H. McLeod. San Francisco: Jossey-Bass, 1988. 61-75.

Haring-Smith, Tori. "The Role of Theory in Advanced Writing and Tutor Training Courses." *Teaching Advanced Composition: Why and How*. Ed. Kate Adams and John Adams. Portsmouth, NH: Boynton, 1991. 151-59.

Haynes, Elizabeth F. "Using Research in Preparing to Teach Writing." *English Journal* 67 (1978): 82-89.

SAC: Speaking Across the Curriculum Newsletter. Ed. Robert O. Weiss. Greencastle, IN: Performing Arts Center, DePauw University.

Sperling, Melanie, and Sarah Warshauer Freedman. "A Good Girl Writes Like a Good Girl: Written Responses to Student Writing." *Written Communication* 4 (1987): 343-69.

Swanson-Owens, Deborah. "Identifying Natural Sources of Resistance: A Case Study of Writing Across the Curriculum." *Research in the Teaching of English* 20 (1986): 69-87.

White, Edward M. *Developing Successful College Writing Programs*. San Francisco: Jossey-Bass, 1989.

Witte, Stephen, and Lester Faigley. *Evaluating College Writing Programs*. Carbondale: Southern Illinois U P, 1983.

Young, Art, and Toby Fulwiler, eds. *Writing Across the Disciplines: Research Into Practice*. Upper Montclair, NJ: Boynton, 1986.

TWELVE

Conclusion

Sustaining Writing Across the Curriculum Programs

MARGOT SOVEN

Several years ago Joseph Williams of the University of Chicago conducted a workshop at La Salle University on writing and critical thinking. The La Salle Writing Across the Curriculum Program was in its fourth year. Fifty faculty members had come out on a cold January evening to hear Williams and returned the next day for a panel presentation by their colleagues on writing assignments that encourage critical thinking. At the end of two very lively days, Williams was asked to sum up. He began by complimenting us for our enthusiasm and energy but ended on a note of incredulity, followed by an ominous prediction: "I am amazed that after four years of writing across the curriculum, you are eager to participate in yet another workshop. By now 'burnout' should be setting in. It's inevitable, so don't be too disappointed when it happens."

As I listened nervously (I had not yet received tenure), I thought, "Could he be right?" Would computer literacy, a hot topic at the time, or a mounting interest in revising the core, or some other campus-wide concern overshadow writing across the curriculum? Would WAC become just another educational fad that had its day,

no doubt to return in 20 years as the brain child of a new generation of academics who thought they had discovered a new idea?
Now in its 10th year, La Salle's WAC program shows no signs
of going under. New faculty seem eager to enroll in our basic
workshop. Last summer we conducted our third follow-up workshop: "Critical Thinking and Writing in Advanced Courses." A
recently approved writing-emphasis course requirement went into
effect in 1990-91, and our Writing Fellows Program is expanding:
We have 25 student tutors and more faculty requests for them than
we can handle. The fifth edition of student essays written in
response to our annual across-the-disciplines writing contest is
ready for distribution, and our faculty manual, *Write to Learn* is
being revised. The biology department has just completed a set of
student materials to augment department workshops on writing,
and three essays on writing, co-authored by faculty, have recently
been published (Morocco and Soven, Simon and Soven, Soven and
Sullivan).

But La Salle is by no means unique. The continuous, vigorous
growth of WAC programs as they approach the end of their first
decade is surprisingly common. Fifteen years after the faculty
seminar at Beaver College, which marked the beginning of writing
across the curriculum as a national movement, many programs
begun during the late seventies and early eighties are remarkably
healthy. Several of those described in this text and many of the
programs reported on in Fulwiler and Young's *Programs that Work*
(e.g., Beaver College, Robert Morris College, and Michigan Technological University) exemplify the staying power of WAC.

Does all this mean that writing across the curriculum (and its
administrators) can look forward to growing old gracefully? Should
we relax and settle back and assume that writing across the curriculum is a permanent campus institution? History would suggest otherwise. As David Russell points out, "cross curricula writing
instruction has never made a permanent impact on academia. . . . Like
other educational reform movements, cross curricula writing instruction was accepted in principle. 'Every teacher should teach
writing' is one of the oldest saws in American academia, but, in
practice reforms were absorbed and transmuted by the system
they resisted" (53). We learn from the past that programs which
challenged traditional departmental structures and the deeply

ingrained assumption that writing is a generalizable skill taught by the English department did not survive. James Kinneavy, who has written extensively on the subject, says it's really too soon to judge the effectiveness of WAC as an educational movement, too early to decide if WAC is "actually a serious attempt to integrate language fully into the curriculum" (375).

However, Kinneavy and Russell do agree that writing across the curriculum enjoys a measure of enthusiastic support from both faculty and administrators unprecedented for programs that cross disciplinary lines. Some of the reasons for that support, described in this text and in numerous essays, are reflected in workshop evaluations such as these:

> Mathmatics Department: The writing project workshop for me was an enlightening experience. Before the workshop, I had never considered using writing assignments as a learning tool in mathematics and physics. Past writing assignments I had given were extra-credit papers, usually on some historical topic, that were designed for those students whose test performance in mathematics were clearly not consistent with their understanding of the material. These assignments were much too loosely defined, however, with the result that most papers were just poor rewrites of encyclopedic accounts. I have much more appreciation now for the care that must go into the assignment. More importantly, I can now envision ways in which writing assignments can be used within the body of the course itself to bolster conceptual understanding of the material.
>
> I was fascinated with the idea of peer review. Coming from a discipline that relies almost exclusively on co-authoring and critiques of colleagues, I would definitely try and institute this. I would sign up for a second workshop on collaborative learning.
>
> The discussion of evaluation of student writing nicely pointed out problems in grading I had never considered. In particular the inefficacy of a large number of comments on a finished paper makes a great deal of sense. For my own future purposes, I would probably go with a rough draft type of assignment that would have significant comments, followed by a chance to act on the comments (DeDio).
>
> Management Department: Prior to attending the workshop, I expected an emphasis on grammar and spelling. I now realize how pointless that would have been.

The workshop was a very good learning experience for me. More importantly, it was very stimulating. It made me think about writing as I haven't thought about writing since Freshman Composition. This kind of workshop requires us to become students again. I think this is very important for me to help me remember the frustration of being taught in a language which I didn't understand. I feel that the need to examine the pedagogy of teaching for me is essential. Too much of my professional experience was "bottom line" oriented. There was very little emphasis on growth (Gauss).

These instructors' remarks, typical of responses from faculty in all disciplines and from institutions of all sorts, underscore the powerful progression of the "first-phase" WAC experience. Faculty come to workshops or request peer tutors because they are concerned about poor student writing, and frustrated by their inability to help. They learn new methods for designing assignments and responding to student papers. But then, the workshop addresses the unexpected, inviting faculty to question long-held assumptions about the function of writing in their classes and the nature of writing in their disciplines. And, as several of our authors have stated, the workshop stimulates faculty to reflect about teaching and renew contact with colleagues. The major value of WAC may very well be, as Fulwiler says, that it "reminds some people why they became college teachers in the first place—before they retreated to separate buildings, isolated offices and competitive research" ("How Well" 121).

Similarly, peer tutoring programs exceed faculty expectations. Initially instructors requesting a peer tutor have a modest objective—a set of papers free from egregious grammatical and spelling errors. Instead they discover they have acquired a collaborator, a partner whose influence extends beyond helping students improve their essays. The peer tutor, trained to question and to encourage students to consider reformulating ideas during the revision process, often changes students' attitudes toward the writing and motivates the faculty sponsor to rethink writing assignments and adopt new methods of responding to student papers.

WHAT NEXT?

To sustain the level of faculty enthusiasm typical of the early stages of a program may be impossible; the epiphany-like effect of new beginnings is hard to replicate. Even to keep a WAC program going in these times of proliferating demands on the college instructor may seem difficult. The challenge facing the WAC administrator who has successfully launched a program is not an easy one. But, as many WAC programs have demonstrated, once faculty have been initiated to WAC, they can be expected to show continued curiosity and commitment—curiosity about new theories and methods of writing instruction and commitment to helping students learn the power of written expression.

The primary task remains the same as it was during the initial phase of the program—to address college teachers' stated needs while introducing fresh areas of inquiry about language. This can mean considering an issue handled in the first workshop in greater depth, for example, focusing second-stage workshops on writing in core courses (see Thaiss, this volume) or writing in advanced courses in the major. These "advanced" workshops can be more theoretically oriented, in contrast to the basic workshop's focus on practical teaching strategies.

Using my own institution as an example once more, the second-stage workshop at La Salle combines several of these goals. The university was in the process of strengthening the program in the major at the same time that faculty concern about students' thinking skills was increasing. We saw the need for a workshop on writing in upper-division courses considered in the context of three contemporary views of critical thinking, e.g., the cognitive, the social-constructionist, and the classical-rhetorical perspectives. Faculty response to this workshop has been positive, although sometimes less ebullient than to the first workshop, and more reflective. As one instructor said, "The workshop was more work than last year. I mean more mental work."

Breaking new ground is always exhilarating, but the WAC director must also consolidate gains if the program is to survive.

Although the benefits of writing as a tool for learning may be obvious to instructors, working with writing takes time, and faculty frustration often resurfaces as students' writing skills do not seem to improve appreciably. Where the faculty training model has been the cornerstone of the program, developing peer tutoring programs or starting a writing center are often the next steps. Both Muriel Harris and Tory Haring-Smith (this volume) underscore the effectiveness of involving students in the writing across the curriculum program. Writing fellows programs and writing centers provide faculty with support, while encouraging faculty and students from all disciplines and levels of capability to feel like members of a community of writers.

It seems that even when the WAC program has been focused on students helping students, as is often the case at major research universities, rather than focused on faculty training, at least some attempt should be made to involve faculty in a dialogue about writing. David Russell does observe that the *shifting responsibility model* of writing instruction based on peer assistance has a better survival rate than the *sharing responsibility model* based on faculty effort (67); however, without some sense of faculty consensus, WAC efforts could be endangered. At schools where the faculty workshop is not really feasible, the freshman interdisciplinary writing course (such as the one at Yale) or collaborative writing courses (such as those at the University of Pennsylvania) are possible approaches for engaging faculty involvement in writing.

Sustaining the writing across the curriculum program also requires reporting its successes and maintaining its visibility. Administrators need to be reminded of what the WAC administrator knows—that something very positive is happening. Documentation in the form of faculty and student surveys is often persuasive. Toby Fulwiler's "Evaluating Writing Across the Curriculum Programs" is an excellent introduction to evaluation methods. Faculty newsletters, student essay contests, and brochures for the admissions office are effective means for communicating and celebrating the benefits of the writing across the curriculum program.

The more ambitious objective of consolidating gains through curriculum revision (such as writing emphasis courses) should be approached with caution. As several of our authors remind us, these courses can imply that responsibility for writing instruction has once more become compartmentalized. However, if writing emphasis courses have special objectives, such as instruction in a particular kind of disciplinary writing, this is less apt to happen. Guidelines for such courses should move beyond page number requirements and statements like "students will have the opportunity to plan and revise."

WHAT ARE THE ROADBLOCKS TO WRITING ACROSS THE CURRICULUM?

What are the possible dangers to WAC if so many positive things are happening? Cynical faculty members who have long ago given up on students and ignore all campuswide efforts to improve teaching? Colleagues in the English department who continue to rehearse old gripes ("Faculty in other departments will never assign enough writing or grade papers properly")? Administrators seeking to cut costs? Yes, each of these groups can pose threats to the WAC program.

But another danger, potentially more serious, is program innovation itself. In "The Danger of Innovations Set Adrift" Edward White describes a series of writing program innovations at different schools, each representing "some strenuous exponents of academic virtue, of energy, of willingness to take risks to achieve worthy ends" that resulted in nothing short of disaster (3). "They [innovations] can be strong forces for ill as well as for good" (5). In each case (the implementation of writing-intensive courses, the expansion of peer tutoring services, the design of a portfolio system for evaluating student writing, the inauguration of a graduation writing test), the cause of failure was imagining that ideas that work well at one institution can be transported to another without considerable attention to the substructures in place at the "model" school. These substructures often involve the availability of human and financial resources, and in the case of the graduation writing test, the careful development of goals. (The most common problem associated with the development of assessment programs is the replacement of goals by means. Beware of proficiency exams as instruments for evaluating writing across the curriculum programs. Instead of strengthening a writing program, they may in fact weaken it, as standards for passing the exam drop to a pragmatic level. What is to be done with the students that fail?) Writing across the curriculum administrators must be clear about their objectives for launching innovation and confident they have secured the necessary resources for an expanded WAC program.

Last, perhaps the most insidious threat to WAC is what David Russell calls the "myth of transience," "the convenient illusion that some new program will cure poor student writing, that there is a single pedagogical solution to complex structural issues" (66). Faculty must be constantly reminded that writing is not a generic skill; the development of writing abilities in different disciplines is a slow process we have only begun to understand. Assigning and responding to writing involves complex understandings about students' capacities and the conventions of and purposes for writing in each discipline. Barbara Walvoord aptly states (this volume), the argument for a permanent commitment to WAC:

> WAC helps people grow. We could have WAC workshops for faculty on every campus every year until the end of the world, because teachers always can be helped by dialogue with colleagues; always need to keep up with new research and theory about writing, thinking, and learning; and always need help in observing and learning what methods will work best in their own classrooms.

We hope the suggestions offered in this text will put the myth of transience to rest. However, once hard-won faculty and administrative support are in place, and programs are launched, it is the writing across the curriculum director who will ultimately be the deciding factor. The hidden danger to writing across the curriculum may not be faculty burnout but writing administrator burnout; the cure is the mutual support and encouragement writing program administrators provide for one another. We present this text in that spirit and look forward to you, our readership, participating in the writing across the curriculum community.

WORKS CITED

DeDio, Richard. Unpublished workshop evaluation. Mathematics Department, La Salle University, Philadelphia, PA, 18 May 1990.

Fulwiler, Toby. "Evaluating Writing Across the Curriculum Programs." *Strengthening Programs for Writing Across the Curriculum.* Ed. Susan McLeod. San Francisco: Jossey-Bass, 1988. 61-75.

———. "How Well Does Writing Across the Curriculum Work?" *College English* 46 (1984): 113-25.

Fulwiler, Toby, and Art Young. eds. *Programs That Work: Models and Methods for Writing Across the Curriculum.* Portsmouth, NH: Boynton/Cook/Heinemann, 1990.

Gauss, Marianne. Unpublished workshop evaluation. Management department, La Salle University, Philadelphia, PA, 18 May 1990.

Kinneavy, James. "Writing Across the Curriculum," *Teaching Composition.* Ed. Gary Tate. Fort Worth: TCU Press, 1987. 353-77.

Morocco, Glenn, and Margot Soven. "Writing Across the Curriculum in the Foreign Language Class." *Hispania* 73 (1990): 845-49.

Russell, David. "Writing Across the Curriculum in Historical Perspective: Toward a Social Interpretation." *College English* 52 (1990): 52-74.

Simon, Barbara, and Margot Soven. "The Teaching of Writing in Social Work Education: A Pressing Priority for the 1990's." *Journal of Teaching Social Work* 3 (1989): 47-63.

Soven, Margot, and William Sullivan. "Demystifying the Academy: Can Exploratory Writing Help?" *Freshman English News* 19 (1990): 13-16.

Soven, Margot. "Beyond the First Workshop: What Else Can You Do to Help Faculty?" *Strengthening Programs for Writing Across the Curriculum.* Ed. Susan McLeod. San Francisco: Jossey-Bass, 1988. 13-20.

White, Edward. "The Damage of Innovations Set Adrift." *AAHE Bulletin* 3 (1990): 3-5.

Wiiliams, Joseph. Keynote speech. Workshop on Critical Thinking and Writing. La Salle University, Philadelphia, PA, 13 January 1985.

Appendix—Starting a WAC Program: Recommended Reading

WAC PRINCIPLES AND DEFINITIONS

Kinneavy, James. "Writing Across the Curriculum." *Teaching Composition: 12 Bibliographical Essays*. Ed. Gray Tate. Fort Worth: Texas Christian UP, 1987. 353-77.

Maimon, Elaine. "Writing in All the Arts and Sciences: Getting Started and Gaining Momentum." *WPA: Writing Program Administration* 4 (Spring 1981): 9-13.

McLeod, Susan. "Defining Writing Across the Curriculum." *WPA: Writing Program Administration* 11 (Fall 1987): 19-24.

Zinnser, William. *Writing to Learn*. New York: Harper, 1988.

CONDUCTING FACULTY WORKSHOPS

Fulwiler, Toby. "Showing, Not Telling, at a Writing Workshop." *College English* 43 (Jan. 1981): 55-63.

———. "Writing Workshops and the Mechanics of Change." *WPA: Writing Programs Administration* 12 (Spring 1989): 7-20.

Herrington, Anne. "Writing to Learn: Writing Across the Disciplines." *College English* 43 (Apr. 1981): 379-87.

WAC STRATEGIES FOR ASSIGNING AND EVALUATING WRITING

Fulwiler, Toby. *The Journal Book*. Portsmouth, NH: Boynton, 1987.

———. *Teaching With Writing*. Upper Montclair, NJ: Boynton, 1987.

Fulwiler, Toby, and Art Young, eds. *Language Connections: Writing and Reading Across the Curriculum*. Urbana, İL: NCTE, 1982.

Griffin, C. Williams, ed. *Teaching Writing in All Disciplines*. San Francisco: Jossey-Bass, 1982.

Holder, Carol, and Andrew Moss. *Improving Student Writing: A Guidebook for Faculty in All Disciplines*. Dubuque, IA: Kendall, 1987.

Walvoord, Barbara Fassler. *Helping Students Write Well: A Guide for Teachers in All Disciplines*. 2nd ed. New York: MLA, 1986.

WAC TEXTBOOKS

Baxerman, Charles. *The Informed Writer*. Boston: Houghton, 1985.

Maimon, Elaine et al. *Writing in the Arts and Sciences*. Cambridge, MA: Winthrop, 1981.

PROGRAM MODELS

Fulwiler, Toby, and Art Young, eds. *Programs That Work: Models and Methods of Writing Across the Curriculum*. Portsmouth, NH: Boynton, 1990.

Thaiss, Christopher, ed. *Writing to Learn: Essays and Reflections on Writing Across the Curriculum*. Dubuque, IA: Kendall, 1983.

PROGRAM EVALUATION

Fulwiler, Toby. "Evaluating Writing Across the Curriculum Programs." *Strengthening Programs for Writing Across the Curriculum*. Ed. Susan McLeod. San Francisco: Jossey-Bass, 1988. 61-75.

———. "How Well Does Writing Across the Curriculum Work?" *College English* 46 (1984): 113-25.

Swanson-Owens, Deborah. "Identifying Natural Sources of Resistance: A Case Study of Implementing Writing Across the Curriculum." *Research in the Teaching of English* 20 (Feb. 1986): 69-97.

Young, Art, and Toby Fulwiler. *Writing Across the Disciplines: Research Into Practice*. Upper Montclair, NJ: Boynton, 1986.

WAC AND THE WRITING PROGRAM

Hilgers, Thomas L., and Joy Marsella. *Making Your Writing Program Work: A Guide to Good Practices*. Newbury Park, CA, 1992.

White, Edward. *Developing Successful College Writing Programs*. San Francisco: Jossey-Bass, 1989.

WAC IN PARTICULAR CONTEXTS

Connolly, Paul, and Teresa Vilardi, eds. *Writing to Learn Mathematics and Science*. New York: Teachers College P, 1989.

Gaudiani, Clair. *Teaching Composition in the Foreign Language Curriculum*. Washington, DC: Center for Applied Linguistics, 1981.

Lutzker, Marilyn. *Research Projects for College Students: What to Write Across the Curriculum*. Westport, CT: Greenwood, 1988.

Martin, Nancy, et al. *Writing and Learning Across the Curriculum 11-17*. Upper Montclair, NJ: Boynton, 1976.

McLeod, Susan, ed. *Strengthening Programs for Writing Across the Curriculum*. San Francisco: Jossey-Bass, 1988.

Stanley, Linda, and Joanna Ambron, eds. *Writing Across the Curriculum in Community Colleges*. San Francisco: Jossey-Bass, 1991.

About the Contributors

Christine Farris is Assistant Professor of English and Women's Studies, Interim Co-Director of the Campuswide Writing Program at Indiana University. She has worked in programs aimed at change since the 1970s when she founded and directed an alternative school. While a poet in the schools for the Teachers' and Writers' Collaborative in New York City, she began her career as a literacy researcher assisting Sylvia Scribner. She has worked as a teacher, consultant, and researcher in WAC programs at the University of Washington and the University of Missouri, where she won the Provost's Outstanding Junior Faculty Award in 1990. She has published articles and book chapters on composition and writing across the curriculum theory, pedagogy, and research.

Joan Graham is Director of the Interdisciplinary Writing Program at the University of Washington. Involved in cross-curriculum program development since 1975, she serves frequently as a consultant to other schools. She is currently writing on course-design issues and co-directing a large research project on university students' writing experience.

Tori Haring-Smith is an Associate Professor in the departments of English and Theatre at Brown University, where she founded the Writing Fellows Program. Her publications include articles on pedagogy, composition, and theater as well as books on collaborative learning, A. A. Milne, the stage history of *The Taming of the*

Shrew, A Guide to Writing Programs and a textbook, *Writing To-gether.* In 1984, she founded the National Conference on Peer Tutoring in Writing, and she directed the consultant-evaluator program for the National Council of Writing Program Administrators from 1986 to 1988. Each year she speaks at numerous conferences and travels to about 25 colleges and universities to conduct faculty workshops on collaborative learning, writing across the curriculum, and critical thinking. She is currently working on *Challenging the Politics of the Classroom,* a book that explores the theory and practice of active learning strategies. In addition to this work, she is a theater director and a mother.

Muriel Harris is Professor of English and Director of the Writing Lab at Purdue University. She edits the *Writing Lab Newsletter*; has authored three textbooks, including the recent *Prentice Hall Reference Guide to Grammar and Usage*; edited *Tutoring Writing, A Sourcebook for Writing Labs*; and authored *Teaching One-to-One: The Writing Conference.* Her journal articles, book chapters, and conference presentations focus on individualized instruction in writing; individualized writing processes; and writing center theory, pedagogy, and administration. She is the recipient of the National Writing Centers' awards for Extraordinary Service to Writing Centers and also for Outstanding Publication.

Peshe C. Kuriloff is the Director of Writing Across the University at the University of Pennsylvania. In addition to working with graduate students and faculty who teach writing-intensive courses in all four undergraduate schools, she also trains and supervises undergraduate writing advisors, directs the graduate student staffed Writing Center, and runs a computer lab. Lately, she has been overseeing development of a new across the curriculum freshman writing seminar program. She has written an advanced composition textbook, *Rethinking Writing,* as well as articles about the pedagogy of teaching writing across the curriculum, the conventions of academic writing, and the relationships between writing across the curriculum and freshman English.

Joyce Neff Magnotto is Professor of English Studies and Chair of the Writing Department at Prince George's Community College where she directed the award-winning Writing Across the Curriculum Program from 1983 to 1991. She serves on the Board of the National Network of WAC programs and as a writing consultant to the U.S. General Accounting Office. Previous publications include articles on WAC and professional development; her current project is a textbook with an emphasis on writing groups. She recently completed her Ph.D. at the University of Pennsylvania where her research addressed cross-disciplinary college writing as social practice.

Susan H. McLeod is Professor of English and Director of Composition at Washington State University, where she also directs the writing across the curriculum faculty seminars and where she recently received an award for excellence in teaching. She consults and conducts workshops on writing across the curriculum at other universities and serves on the Board of Consultants of the National Network of Writing Across the Curriculum Programs. Her publications include *Writing About the World*, a WAC reader for freshman composition; *Strengthening Programs for Writing Across the Curriculum*; and articles on writing across the curriculum, emotions and the writing process, and writing program administration. She is currently working on a book-length study of the affective domain and the writing process.

Linda H. Peterson is Director of Undergraduate Studies in English and Co-Director of the Bass Writing Program at Yale University. She is co-editor of the *Norton Reader* (8th edition) and a new critical edition of *Wuthering Heights*, as well as author of numerous essays about Victorian literature and about teaching of writing. With her colleague Leslie E. Moore, she taught a version of the freshman course she describes in this volume, now a regular offering in the English department's curriculum.

Karen Wiley Sandler is Associate Professor of French and Vice President and Dean of Academic Affairs at Juniata College in Huntington, Pennsylvania. She received her Ph.D. in Romance Language from the University of Pennylvania and began her teaching career at the University of Vermont in the Department of Romance Languages, where she taught all levels of French language and literature, comparative literature, and secondary teaching methods. She left full-time teaching after 16 years at the University of Vermont to become Assistant to the Associate Provost at Gettysburg College, where she also taught an introductory, interdisciplinary course for first-year students as well as Intermediate French. She moved to her current position in 1989. Her research interests include Montaigne, Louise Labé, Marguerite de Navarre, and the use of writing in the teaching of foreign languages and literature. She is also the co-author (with Susan O. Whitebook) of an intermediate review grammar, *Tour de Grammaire* .

Raymond Smith was born in Charlottesville, Virginia, and was educated at the University of Virginia and the University of Missouri-Columbia. In 1985, on a whim, he served as a Research Assistant for the Campus Writing Program, a new WAC program at the University of Missouri-Columbia. While working in this capacity he discovered that he was as interested in other disciplines as much as his own (English Renaissance literature). He served as Assistant Director of the Campus Writing Program at the University of Missouri for two years and then as Director in 1989. Since 1990, he has directed the Campus-wide Writing Program at Indiana University, where he works with faculty from a variety of disciplines to find profitable ways to use writing in their courses. He also administers Writing Tutorial Services, Indiana University's writing center.

Margot Soven is Associate Professor of English at La Salle University. She directs the La Salle University Writing Project, the Writing Fellows Program, and is Co-Director of the Freshman Composition Program. She serves on the Board of Consultants of the National Network of Writing Across the Curriculum Programs and is a Consultant-Evaluator for the Council of Writing Program Administrators. She has published articles on both freshman composition and writing across the curriculum. For the past 15 years, she has conducted workshops on the teaching of writing on both high school and college campuses.

Barbara R. Stout is Professor of English and Chair of the Department of English Composition and Literature at Montgomery College in Rockville, Maryland. She directed the Writing Across the Curriculum program there from 1983 to 1991. She was Co-Founder and Co-Director of the National Capitol Area Writing Project. She gives workshops and publishes articles about writing across the curriculum and curricular innovations at community colleges.

Christopher Thaiss directs the Composition and Writing Across the Curriculum Programs at George Mason University, where he is Associate Professor of English. Active in the development of cross-curricular writing in schools and colleges since 1978, Thaiss also coordinates the National Network of Writing Across the Curriculum Programs and works with teachers in the elementary, middle, and high schools through the Northern Virginia Writing Project. Books he has written or edited include *Writing to Learn: Essays and Reflections, Speaking and Writing, K-12* (with Charles Suhor), *Language Across the Curriculum in the Elementary Grades*, and a composition textbook, *Write to the Limit*. Current projects include a composition anthology (*A Sense of Value*) and a book on youth baseball.

Barbara E. Walvoord is Director of Writing Across the Curriculum and Professor of English at the University of Cincinnati. She has also initiated and directed writing across the curriculum programs at Loyola College in Maryland and at Central College in Pella, Iowa. She was Co-Founder and for several years Co-Director of the Maryland Writing Project, an affiliate of the National Writing Project. She was also Co-Founder and Director of the Baltimore Area Consortium for Writing Across the Curriculum (BACWAC). In *Thinking and Writing in College* (NCTE) she and five collaborators report their naturalistic research into college students' thinking and writing in four disciplines. In addition, she has published two textbooks and a book for teachers—*Helping Students Write Well: A Guide for Teachers in All Disciplines* (MLA) as well as numerous articles and and has given numerous conference presentations. She regularly does consulting and workshops on writing and critical thinking at colleges across the nation and is a member of the Board of Consultants of the National Network of WAC Programs.